Tropical
Tastes

Warm memories
of the Florida Keys

Carol G⸺ 1993

Tropical
Tastes

And Tantalizing Tales

Carol Garvin

Valiant Press

Valiant Press, Inc.
P.O. Box 330568, Miami, FL 33233

The following individuals have generously given permission to include recipes and information: "Alice's Borrowed Molasses Snaps," by Alice Peltier; "Avocado Bread," by Barbara Roberts; "Chicken Broth," "Chocolate Peanut Butter Delights," "Fresh Coconut Cake," "Lime Jello Salad," "Lobster Bisque," "Sand Dollar Pie," and "Traditional Key Lime Pie," by Hilda Hunt; "Chicken Cacciatore A La Trigg Adams," by J. Trigg Adams; "Clare's Fresh Mango Bread," by Clare Gray; "Fast Eddie's Macho Male Eggplant Stirfry," by Edward C. Gurney, Jr.; "Hodge Podge Ceasar Salad," by Matt and Sheila Kuhl; "Hot Artichoke Dip," and "Hot Spinach Dip," by Sally Matluck Boisseau; "Mud Puppy Mousse," "Sweet and Sour Dressing," and "Tom Wiles Spinach Salad," by Becky Wiles; "Seafood Crêpes," by Sheila Kuhl; "Sky Fried Squirrel," by Marie Crawford; "Small Dog Small Rope Quiche," by Darlene Dodge; "Snap Cackle And Pop (oven fried)," by Leslie Garvin-Owen; "Ten Thousand Islands (Cheese Buttons)," by Darlene Jarvi; and "Wild Plant Recipes," by Roger L. Hammer.

Library of Congress Cataloging-in-Publication Data
Garvin, Carol.
    Tropical tastes and tantalizing tales / Carol Garvin.
       p.   cm.
    Includes index.
    ISBN 0-9633461-1-3
    1. Cookery. 2. Florida—Miscellanea. I. Title.
TX714.G365 1993
641.5—dc20
                                                      93-7154
                                                       CIP

Front Cover and Illustrations by Carol Garvin

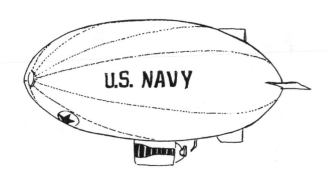

Lovingly For My Parents

William F. Hunt
Hilda Chury Hunt

Contents

Acknowledgment of Thanks

To all of my family and friends, who contributed by sending recipes, sharing ideas, or by just listening.

To Charity Johnson my publisher, who because I can't type, toiled endlessly over a completely handwritten manuscript. I know at times my eccentricities caused her much anxiety and probably a few gray hairs.

To my dear friend Gail Renard, for proofreading, final editing, and spicing up the copy.

To Barbara Roberts, who's faith never wavered for a moment, her early morning calls guided my path.

To my cousin Darlene Dodge, who over a bottle of wine got me to pull this project out of the closet, then graciously shared her kitchen for unremitting experiments.

To my mother Hilda Hunt, who went back into her memory bank to supply me with childhood favorites.

To Sheila Kuhl and Greg Feldman, who were never without an opinion.

To Roger Hammer, who advised me on wild things.

To Ann Cooper of Dade Cooperative Extention, for providing me with names, phone numbers, and reams of information.

To Don Pybas of Sea Grant, for advice, pamphlets, information, and a fine friendship.

To Beth, Jan, and J.E., who taste tested the alcoholic beverages and then provided some of the most creative recipe names.

To Cindy Russell, who advised me on snakes, gators, and other wild delights.

To Tipi Punnett, who lives on the Caribbean island of St. Vincent, for providing me with the photo of the Bequia Sailing Regatta which graces the cover.

And last, but not least, to my loyal canine companions Wooky and Gator, the official cookbook taste testers, who with accusing eyes dealt with the failures and with great enthusiasm consumed the leftover successes.

Introduction

Most of you all who know me, know me for my watercolors of Florida and the Caribbean islands. This is just one side of Carol Garvin. The desire to create seeks many outlets and is not limited to the drawing board.

Some of my most satisfying moments have been spent in the kitchen. There is nothing more stimulating than asking a dangerous man to tea. If because I'm an artist, you're expecting tofu and sprouts, you'll be profoundly disappointed, for this book is replete with the simple, the exotic, and the forbidden.

Join me and wander these pages for good food, humor, tales of Florida history and habitat, and perhaps even adventure. Guaranteed to entertain . . . whether you are a native, a visitor, or just thinking of asking someone dangerous to tea.

Carol Garvin
Coconut Grove, FL
1993

Getting Under Way

Liquid Sustenance
and
Appetizers

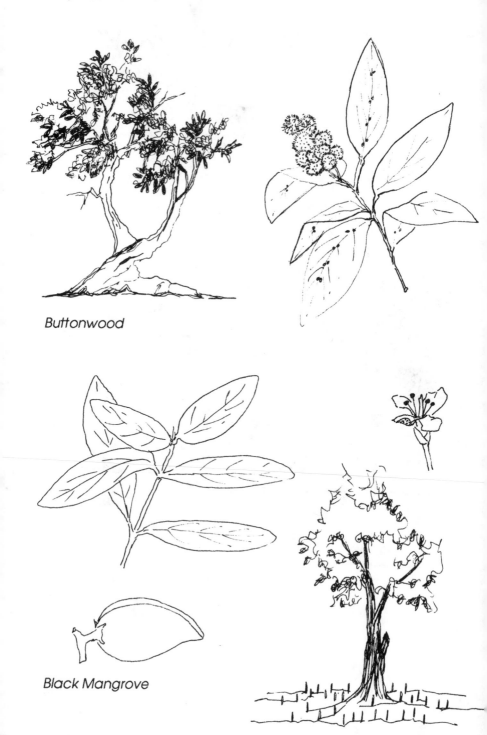

Buttonwood

Black Mangrove

Mangroves

Mangroves are simply land plants that have adapted to living in a harsh marine environment. That in itself is hardly simple.

Florida's abundant marine life is directly related to her red mangrove nurseries, where life begins and flourishes in these protective hatcheries.

A healthy, producing mangrove swamp drops more than three tons of leaves per acre each year. Micro-organisms, tiny fish, and the like, feed on the decaying leaves. These creatures are then eaten by higher life forms, which, in their turn, are consumed by higher ones, resulting in a food chain ending with man.

If you are a hardy soul who also enjoys quiet and solitude, I urge you to explore a mangrove swamp. You'll need your old sneakers, socks, long pants, long-sleeved shirt, and insect repellent—just in case. And be sure to take along an old croaker sack also known as a burlap bag, because mangroves are a beachcomber's paradise.

A word of caution: beware of muddy areas. You could lose a shoe. Oh yes, the age-old question, asked wide-eyed and with great trepidation, always arises. "Are there snakes in there?" In all my years of swamp-tromping, and they are considerable, I've only seen one. Harmless. He took off in the opposite direction like a scalded cat. Actually, I'm more concerned about broken glass.

There are four types of mangroves: red, white, black, and buttonwood. None of these is related. Of the four, red mangroves are the celebrities, and it's this type we visualize when we think of mangroves. They are the only ones with arching prop roots. These aerial roots have an aeration system that allows the tree to live in its watery environment. They are also a catchall for debris, giving the mangrove its reputation as an island builder.

Another unique feature of the red mangrove is its cigar-shaped seedling or propagule. Once the tree drops them, these propagules are carried along in the current horizontally until the root tip becomes waterlogged. Then the seedling slowly rotates into a vertical position. Eventually, it will go aground in calm, shallow water and take root. And, island building begins anew.

A sure sign of a healthy, producing mangrove swamp are lush grassbeds directly offshore. These provide a natural habitat for sea life, promote clear water, and restrict bottom damage from tides or extreme weather.

Ironically, the unique qualities of the pioneering red mangrove have been its undoing. They colonize the coast and feed the fish, which attract the people, who want to develop the land where the mangroves live.

White Mangrove

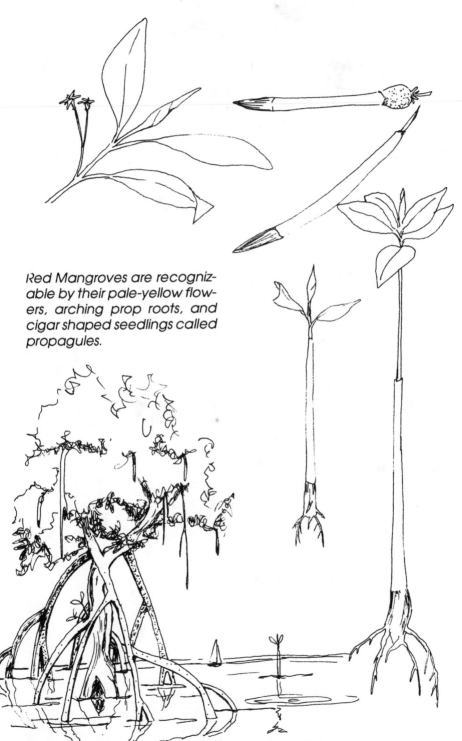

Red Mangroves are recognizable by their pale-yellow flowers, arching prop roots, and cigar shaped seedlings called propagules.

Red Mangrove Tea

Pour boiling water over dried red mangrove leaves. Let steep 5 minutes. Flavor as desired. Serve iced or hot.

Wild Red Bay Tea*

Red Bay or Sweet Bay is a native tree. The leaves can be substituted for bay leaves in soups, stews, and meats.

Boil dried leaves for 15-20 minutes, then allow to steep for a while. Especially good iced.

CAUTION:

*Know your wild plants. If you are adventuresome but untutored, call Dade County Parks and Recreation, (305) 257-1631. Their resident naturalist, Roger Hammer, is an authority on wild things. His charismatic personality and vast knowledge of our native plants make his tours fun, informative, and entertaining.

Wild Pennyroyal Tea

Pennyroyal is a native mint found in the piney woods. It is 6 inches to 2 feet high, a low, spreading plant with 3/8-inch-long needle-like leaves sprouting from brittle hairy stems topped with fuzzy tufts of minute lavender flowers. Crushed leaves are very aromatic. Again, don't do this without expert guidance. Recommended reading is a book by Julia F. Morton, Ph.D., "Wild Plants for Survival in South Florida."

Steep sprigs in boiling water about 20 minutes. Serve hot or iced. Flavor as desired.

Shell Ginger Tea

Ellen Bain, a friend who went to the Bahamas on vacation and stayed ten years, called this a typical "bush tea." This is a common dooryard ornamental plant, Alpinia speciosa, also called Shell Flower.

4   leaves (about 2 feet long) dried or fresh
1   quart water

Cut leaves with scissors into 2 inch sections. Boil 20 minutes with a lid on. Allow to steep for a while. Serve hot or iced.

Key West Coffee

Serves 1

If you have dined al fresco in Key West, in a lush tropical garden, or by the turquoise-blue sea, and sipped their fragrant cinnamon coffee as I have, this simple recipe will re-create that charming memory.

1   cup coffee
Cream or sugar (optional)
1   cinnamon stick

1. Prepare 1 cup of coffee the way you like it.
2. Add 1 stick of cinnamon.
3. Relax and enjoy!

Key Limeade

Yields 1/2 gallon

2/3 cup fresh Key lime* juice
2/3 cup sugar (or more)
1/2 gallon water

Combine all ingredients in a large container, sweeten to taste. Serve over ice.

*If Key limes are not available, substitute local limes.

The Legend of Ned Pent

The incorrigible spirit of Ned Pent made him a legend around Biscayne Bay. Perhaps I favor him because he homesteaded the land on which my Coconut Grove house now stands.

Born in Florida in 1830, Ned descended from Bahamian seafarers. He was once a barefoot mailman, and though he had taken a homestead like his kinsmen before him, Ned's life was forever interwoven with the sea. He established a reputation in the Biscayne Bay area as an able boat builder and sailor.

Because of his carpentry skills, he was often called upon to build coffins, a job he considered loathsome. As time went by, Ned became more and more uncooperative about building coffins for the small community. The most workable solution was to provide him with the necessary lumber and a jug of liquor, and lock him in his boat shop for the night. By morning, the job was complete.

Eventually, even this strategy went awry. While bracing himself for one of these unpleasant tasks, he managed to become a little too well-oiled. The next morning, Ned and his empty jug were found lying beside a well-made coffin, complete with centerboard.

He may have had a weakness for "low bush lightning," but he certainly had a strong constitution. On a Christmas sailing trip, while indulging in continuous holiday merrymaking, Ned fell overboard and disappeared. A cold front came through and several days elapsed. About the time he was given up for lost, he was found beached on a sand bank—sleeping peacefully, well fortified with spirits, and seemingly no worse for the wear.

Sozon's Cone Shell

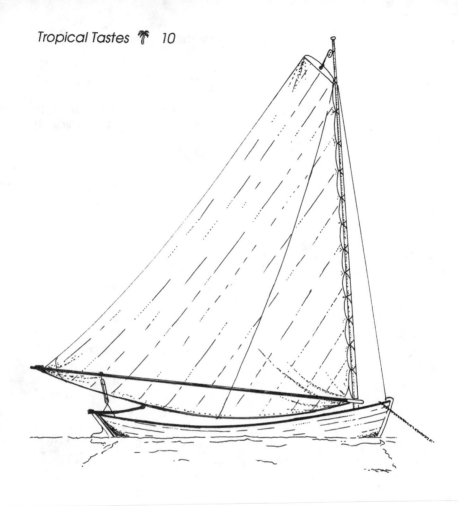

Low Bush Lightning

Serves 20

1/2 gallon dark rum
2 liter bottle ginger ale
48 ounce bottle cran-raspberry cocktail
1/2 gallon orange juice
6 ounce container frozen limeade concentrate, undiluted
5 pound hunk dry ice—call your local ice house

Using a very large bowl—about 4 gallons—pour in all ingredients except ice. You may want to split the ice with an ice pick using 1/2 at a time. It bubbles and boils like a witch's brew. Smoke rolls out of the bowl like something from a horror movie. It's fun, tastes good, and looks irresistible. It is also extremely potent, so beware. The dry ice is harmless and evaporates into the air.

Coral Snake
(A Frozen Drink)

Serves 4

1/4   cup frozen orange/raspberry concentrate, undiluted (Tropicana brand)
1/4-1/2 cup dark rum
1/4   cup Triple Sec
1   tray ice cubes or fill blender 2/3 to 3/4 full
Garnish optional—lemon slices and any dark purple fruit such as dark purple grapes, blackberries, blueberries.

Combine all ingredients except garnishes in a blender. Whiz until slushy and all cubes are gone. Put a slice of lemon on edge of glass and purple fruit on top to represent all colors of the snake. Consume and wait for the "bite"! Store in freezer.

How to Eat a Mango, Al Green's Way

Cut the mango in half, remove seed. Scoop out center, pour in rum, brandy, or the liquor of your choice. Drink the contents. Throw the mango away.

Sinful Mango Smoothee

Serves 4

A friend who owns a tropical nursery in Miami, gave me this recipe, sans rum. Naturally, not being able to leave well enough alone, I had to "improve" it.

1   cup Half and Half
1   cup mango slices
1   tablespoon Key lime juice (optional)
1   cup crushed ice
2-3 jiggers rum

Pour Half and Half and mango slices in blender. Blend at high speed until smooth. Add remaining ingredients. Serve immediately.

Bathtub Amaretto

Yields 1 1/2 cups

1/4 cup water
1/2 cup sugar
3/4 cup vodka
1/2 teaspoon almond extract
2   tablespoons almond slivers

1.   In a sauce pan boil sugar and water until the sugar dissolves and the syrup becomes clear. Set aside to cool.
2.   In a 10 ounce bottle (seltzer bottles work well) pour cooled syrup, vodka, extract, and almonds. Cap, turn a few times to mix. Store in a cupboard one week.

Sea Hare—large shelless snails found grazing on flats, which exude a purple ink when handled.

Colombian Brew
(Refajo)

Serves 2

This is a favorite drink of the Colombian "campesino." During my first visit, I was served this beverage in a small, open restaurant high in the mountains. I ordered rabbit because I wanted a true Colombian experience. I got one! We were sitting under a chickee surrounded by aralia hedge. After taking my order, the chef promptly dispatched the rabbit on the other side of the hedge. I drank copious amounts of "refajo." The poor rabbit? It was delicious.

1   bottle Colombiana (an orange-colored creme-soda-like soft drink) or Jamaican Kola
1   can beer

Mix 50/50. Serve crackling cold over ice.

Traditional Rum Punch

Serves 1

1   of sour
2   of sweet
3   of strong
4   of weak

Translation:
1   part lime juice
2   parts sugar
3   parts rum
4   parts water

Mix all of above over ice cubes. Find a comfortable chair or chaise lounge with a view which appeals to you and settle back. After one of these you won't be able to move for a while.

*Cattle Egrets
have yellow
beaks and legs.*

Dracula's Blood
(A Frozen Drink)

Serves 4

1/4   cup undiluted orange/raspberry frozen concentrate (Tropicana brand)
1/4   cup undiluted piña colada frozen concentrate
1/2   cup dark rum
2   tablespoons Chambord plus 4 teaspoons (raspberry liqueur)
2/3-3/4   blender ice cubes
Maraschino cherries
Slivered almonds

1.   Combine both concentrates, rum, 2 tablespoons Chambord, ice cubes in a blender and whiz until slushy.
2.   Pour into glasses. Top with maraschino cherry, two almond slivers (Dracula's teeth), and gently pour on top about 1 teaspoon Chambord. Store in freezer.

Frozen Strawberry Daiquiri

Yields about 1 quart

16 ounce box frozen strawberries
2/3 cup rum
1 tablespoon sugar
3 or more cups ice cubes

1. Blenderize all ingredients until slushy.
2. Serve immediately. Store in freezer.

Fresh Frozen Key Lime Daiquiri

Yields about 1 quart

2 Key limes or limes available in your area
6 tablespoons sugar
3 or more cups ice cubes
3/4 cup rum

1. Grate the peel off one lime, then halve both limes and juice them.
2. Blenderize juice, grated peel, sugar, rum, and cubes until slushy.
3. Serve immediately. Store in freezer.

Queen Conch

The Queen Conch (Strombus gigas)

The queen conch (pronounced konk) is a large tropical marine snail, better known for its lovely pink shell than for its excellent flavor. Native to the warm Caribbean Sea, it has always been a reliable source of protein for islanders. At one time, so much conch was being consumed in Nassau, the vast number of shells being dumped into the harbor were creating a navigational hazard. Fines were finally imposed to curtail the activity.

Young conch grow four to six inches in the first two years. Juveniles have a spiral or cone-like shell and are known as rollers. At four years of age, they begin to form the flaring iridescent, rose-colored lip, a signal to other conch that they are sexually mature. When fully grown, they are eight to twelve inches long and can weigh up to five pounds. Over-harvesting has made it difficult to judge the conch's natural life span, but unmolested, it is thought they may live as long as twenty-five years.

Conch are usually found in the turtle grass beds, foraging for algae. Conch fishing, Bahamian style, is done from a dinghy with the aid of a glass-bottom bucket and a conch hook, a long pole with two metal tines on one end, bent at a ninety degree angle to the pole. When a conch is seen on the sea floor through the "water glass," the hook is lowered and the tines carefully slipped under the unsuspecting mollusk. Raising the pole hand over hand, the hook is brought to the surface with its prize.

The conch can produce a lustrous pink pearl, but though rare, the jewel does not command a high price. Unfortunately, like the conch shell's rosy lip, the pearl will eventually fade from exposure to the sun.

Conch The Aphrodisiac

Conch cleaning in the Bahamas takes on a rather festive air, mainly because Bahamian men believe conch contains an aphrodisiac. What they are after is a clear gelatinous protein rod called a "crystalline style," which they call the "pistol." You will hear them say, "Give me de pistol, mon," or "I got de pistol, mon."

This rod is a few inches long and is contained in a sheath which ends at the conch's stomach. Inside the conch, it aids digestion. Inside a man, it's supposed to do other things.

This is why you always see groups of Bahamian men enthusiastically cleaning conch. First, there is the initial struggle for the pistol. Once he's seized it, the victor tilts back his head, dangles the prize over his open mouth, and swallows the slender, quivering rod raw.

The effect is instantaneous. He displays a broad, knowing, triumphant grin. As for its other effects, I don't know. I only know it makes them grin.

De-conching the Shell

There are many ways to remove a conch from its shell. The easiest method is to freeze the entire animal, shell and all, overnight. In the morning, submerge the shell in a bucket of water for a couple of hours to thaw it. Using a pair of pliers, firmly grip the operculum (the stiff, brown, front door attached to the bottom of the conch's foot), and gently ease the conch from its shell. Not only does this method give an undamaged shell, but freezing aids in tenderizing the conch. Soaking your empty shell in water, adding a little bleach, will dispel any fishy odor that might linger.

Cleaning the Conch

If this is your first time, I suggest you gather reinforcements. There may be times during this procedure that you will need advice or encouragement to press on.

Set yourself up outside near a water source. Uncap a bottle of vinegar or have some lime juice ready in a bowl.

Pick up the conch by the operculum and have a good look. You do not want to cut off the operculum, because it provides a handle with which to grip the slippery creature throughout the ordeal.

Separating the edible foot from the other parts is almost instinctive. No one in their right mind would eat any of the slimy stuff. Just cut it all away. Next, off with the eyes and snout. Peel or pare the skin off the foot and there it is, the snow-white edible steak.

Hold on! You're not finished. Carefully feel the colorful orange mantle for your hidden pearl. It could be your lucky day. Now you may cut off the operculum, but don't throw it away. After it dries, glue it to a piece of cotton and place it back in the shell so it looks as if the conch is still at home. Shells without opercula are less valuable.

Now what about all that slime on your hands and tools? Relax. It will come off with the lime juice or vinegar. Congratulations, you're done! Now you know why conch is so expensive.

Bruising the Conch

"Bruising" is West Indian vernacular for tenderizing. Conch is extremely tough, and tenderizing it is a must unless you are blenderizing it to make chowder. Bruising conch, West Indian style, means pounding it out flat with a soda-pop bottle to twice its original size.

Florida Laws

It is illegal to harvest conch in Florida. You'll have to get the imported item from a seafood market. You won't get the pearl, or the "pistol," but you won't get the fine either!

Bahama Style Conch Hook

Fighting Conch

Lacy Lambie
(Cracked Conch)

Serves 4-6

4   conch, pounded until thin and lacy
1   cup buttermilk
Lime juice
Salt and pepper
Worcestershire sauce
Flour
1   egg
1   tablespoon milk
Cracker meal
Oil
Lime wedges

1.   Pound out conch until thin and lacy—at least twice its normal size. Cut into two-inch pieces. Soak in buttermilk about 1 hour to remove some of the "conchiness."
2.   Remove from buttermilk, shake off. Sprinkle with lime juice, salt, pepper, and Worcestershire sauce. Roll in flour.
3.   Combine egg and milk. Dip conch in it, then roll in cracker meal. Fry conch in about 1/2 inch hot oil over medium-high heat until golden. Keep warm until served.
4.   Serve with cocktail sauce, Tiger Sauce, garlic butter, or your favorite dipping sauce and lime wedges.

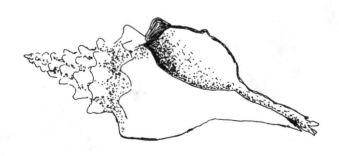

Horse Conch (carnivorous)

Pickled Purple Passion
(Pickled Eggs)

Yields 12

12	hard-boiled eggs, peeled
2 1/2-3	cups cider vinegar
1	can beets with juice
1	medium onion, sliced
1	box pickling spices

1. Put the eggs in a bowl large enough to hold all the above ingredients.
2. In a sauce pan, heat the last four ingredients, but do not boil. Pour over eggs.
3. Cover and refrigerate. Let sit at least 24 hours. Good snack food, convenient on beach outings and day sails.

Sea Urchin

Roasted Peanuts in the Shell

Serves 6

1 bag raw peanuts in the shell

1. Preheat oven to 300° F.
2. Spread unshelled raw peanuts on a large cookie sheet. Bake for 35-40 minutes. Stir frequently.
3. Serve warm—preferably outside so people can throw the shells over their shoulders. After all, this is half the fun.

Deviled Eggs

Yields 24 stuffed eggs

12 hard-boiled eggs
Salt and pepper to taste
3 tablespoons sweet relish
1/2 teaspoon yellow mustard
4-5 tablespoons mayonnaise
Paprika

1. Slice eggs in half lengthwise and scoop yolks into a small mixing bowl. Mash yolks with a pastry cutter or fork.
2. Stir all remaining ingredients except paprika into yolks, until smooth.
3. Fill eggs with yolk mixture and sprinkle paprika lightly on top for color.
4. Serve cold.

Cloaked and Daggered Water Chestnuts

Serves 4

1 can whole water chestnuts
Sliced bacon
Light brown sugar
Shredded coconut
Pineapple chunks (1 small can)
Wooden toothpicks

1. Preheat oven to 350° F.
2. Drain chestnuts and roll on paper towel to remove excess water.
3. Roll chestnuts in brown sugar, then wrap bacon once around chestnut, trim off excess bacon. Roll in coconut, top with pineapple chunk secured to chestnut with wooden toothpick. One strip of bacon will wrap 3 or 4 chestnuts.
4. Bake chestnuts on broiler pan or on a rack in pan about 20 minutes or until bacon is brown and crispy. Serve hot.

Saw Palmetto

Peppery Hot Spinach Dip

Serves 4

3   pounds fresh spinach
2/3 cup grated extra sharp cheddar cheese (Cracker Barrel)
2/3 cup grated jalapeño jack cheese
2/3 cup grated Muenster cheese
1/3 cup Lipton's dried onion soup mix
1/3 cup sour cream

1.   Preheat oven to 325° F.
2.   Fill your largest mixing bowl with cold water. Pour spinach in, agitate with your hands. This causes the sand (which lives in spinach) to sink. Lift out spinach, empty bowl. Repeat, filling, washing—3 times if necessary.
3.   Pour the spinach in a large pot. Using only the water which clings to the leaves, cover and steam until done—about 2 minutes. You will be amazed at how much raw spinach cooks down. Drain.
4.   Chop spinach. Blend spinach with cheeses. Add onion soup mix to sour cream, combine with spinach mixture.
5.   Pour into oven-proof bowl. Bake 35-40 minutes. Serve warm with tostada chips and ice cold beer.

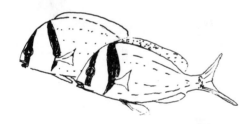

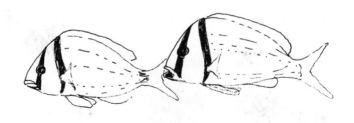

Pork fish are silver with a yellow head and tail, and distinctive black stripies.

Sally's Heart of Artichoke Dip

Serves 4

Sally, an excellent cook and founder of Citizens Against Pet Overpopulation (CAPO), lives in a quaint tropical home perched on the banks of New River in Ft. Lauderdale. While "softening up" her guests with epicurean delights, her canine co-conspirator waits patiently in the wings. When your guard is totally relaxed, Sally gives the secret signal. Almost casually, out saunters a shaggy creature with the most appealing demeanor, now groomed to perfection and looking for a home.

15 ounce can artichoke hearts in water
2/3 cup grated Kraft Parmesan cheese
2/3 cup mayonnaise

1. Preheat oven to 350° F.
2. Drain and chop artichokes.
3. Blend all ingredients well. Spread in an 8 inch pie dish.
4. Bake 30 minutes. Serve warm with Carr's Table Crackers.

Smoked Fish Dip

Yields 3 cups

12   ounces cream cheese (1 1/2 eight ounce packages)
1/2   cup sour cream
2   tablespoons milk
5   teaspoons lime juice
1   tablespoon parsley
2   tablespoons onion, chopped
2 1/2   cups smoked fish

1. In a large mixing bowl combine all ingredients. Blend well with an electric mixer.
2. Chill. Serve with crackers.

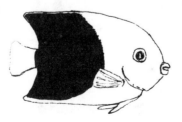

Four Alarm Hot Pepper Jelly

Yields seven 1/2 pint jars

This is an easy and delicious appetizer. Simply spread cream cheese on melba toast and top with this tangy jelly.

1/2	cup fresh chili peppers
3/4	cup green pepper
1 1/2	cups cider vinegar
6 1/2	cups sugar
6	ounce package liquid pectin (Certo)
4	drops Tabasco Sauce (optional)

Red or green food coloring (optional)

CAUTION: Use gloves when touching chili peppers and don't rub your eyes. It will be painful.

1. Removing seeds from hot peppers is optional. Seeds make it hotter. I leave them in.
2. Blenderize hot peppers, green pepper, and vinegar. Pour into a large sauce pan. Bring to a boil over medium heat, add sugar. Cook, stirring until sugar is dissolved.
3. Remove from heat. Let cool 5 minutes, then stir in Certo, Tabasco, and food color of your choice. Pour into sterilized jars. Cap or cover with paraffin. Cool. Tighten cap.

Ten Thousand Islands

(Cheese Buttons)

Yields 4 to 5 dozen

This recipe came from my cousin Darlene who lives in Naples. It's wonderful.

1	cup (2 sticks) margarine, softened
2 1/2	cups sharp cheddar cheese, grated
2	cups flour
2	cups Rice Krispies

Pecan halves

1. Preheat oven to 375° F.
2. In a large mixing bowl mix margarine with cheese. Add flour, blend well. Stir in Rice Krispies.
3. Roll into walnut-sized balls. Place on cookie sheet and flatten. Press a pecan half in the center.
4. Bake 20 minutes. Serve warm.

Bleu Moon

Serves 10-12

8   ounce package creamed cheese
6   ounce package Bleu cheese
1/2 teaspoon cider vinegar
1/2 teaspoon Dijon mustard
1/4 teaspoon Worcestershire sauce
1/2 cup chopped walnuts

1.   Combine softened cheeses, add remaining ingredients except nuts. Chill 1 hour.
2.   Form a ball. Roll in nuts. Chill. Serve with wheat crackers.

Gator Bites

Serves 4

Alligators are protected in Florida. Poaching gator is a third-degree felony with fines up to 5,000 dollars and/or one year in jail. There is a very limited season in September with a select number of permits issued through the Florida Game and Freshwater Fish Commission. Gator meat is available at seafood markets. Choice cuts come from the tail and jaws. Body and leg meat requires removal of white tendons and vessels. All cuts require complete removal of fat and sinew. Gators play a key role in Everglades ecology by digging out small ponds sustaining a myriad of wildlife during the dry season. Since I understand their essential role in the environment and because I find beauty in their calm brown eyes, I prefer them in ponds, rather than on my plate. However, I include it for the pioneering types.

1 pound gator meat
Parsley flakes
Salt and pepper
Cracker crumbs
Oil

1.   Prepare meat as suggested above, cut into bite-sized pieces. Season, roll
in cracker meal. Fry in hot oil about 5 minutes. Beware, gator can get tough.
Serve with Louisiana Hot Sauce, or sweet and sour sauce, or Braswell's Hot
Tomato Relish.

Coontie

Sandspur

Provisioning Details
Bread and Soup

The Banana (Musa paradisiaca)

The palm-like banana "tree" is neither palm nor tree. It's a giant herb, ranking second to the coconut in tropical economic importance.

A native of Asia, the banana was brought to the tropical Americas by the conquistadors. It was commercially introduced to the United States in 1870 by a Cape Cod sea captain who had received two stalks as a parting gift from a Jamaican planter. Its exotic taste and appearance created such a sensation that he began importing bananas on a grand scale. By 1885, he had formed the Boston Fruit Company, which would eventually evolve into the United Fruit Company.

Banana plants are cold-sensitive and can die back to the ground if hit by frost. However, as warm weather returns, young plants will spring up from the root stock. Highly prized as ornamental plants, they will grow as far north as coastal South Carolina. There they are planted lovingly next to chimneys in hopes that warmth from the fireplaces will furnish them some degree of protection during the winter.

There are countless types of bananas, varying in size, color, and degree of sweetness, but the ripeness of the fruit determines its ultimate use. They are one of the few fruits that may be harvested green and stored without impairing the flavor.

A banana cannot keep a secret. It will always let you know what's going on inside by the color of the peel. When banana peels are green, or pale yellow and green tipped, the pulp is firm and starchy. It can be served broiled, baked, or fried as a vegetable.

When the peel is a uniform yellow, having only a trace of green on the tips, the pulp is still firm, and eighty to ninety percent of the starch has been converted to fruit sugars. It may be served as above.

A yellow peel with brown flecks covers a pulp that is fully ripe. Almost 100 percent of the starch has been converted to fruit sugars. Use this as fresh fruit.

If the peel is a uniform brown color, the pulp is semi-soft and overripe. These bananas make superior cakes, breads, and cookies. Actually, I like them fried. If you don't have the nerve to cook this banana, you're making a big mistake, but read on.

A banana with a dark brown to black peel covers very soft pulp. Lovingly lay this banana to rest in your staghorn fern basket. Honest. In about a week the banana will turn the fern a deep rich green and your staghorns will love you for it.

Refrigeration is the only way to slow down the ripening process. The peel will turn brown, but it won't harm the flavor. Peeled and frozen, bananas make wonderful popsicles.

During baking, banana leaves can be used as a substitute for aluminum foil, imparting a delicate flavor to the food. They also make great emergency rain capes, but look out for the sap stains.

There is an unwritten law in banana circles: Never mess with your banana plants when you're wearing your good clothes. However, if you've had a sap accident and some mystifying tan-colored stains appear (you won't know until after the clothes have been washed), this is supposed to work: Mix equal parts of liquid chlorine bleach, borax, and water. Apply this to the stain a few drops at a time and let it stand a while. Rinse with some cold water. (Remember, always consider color and fabric type when using bleach.) Good luck!

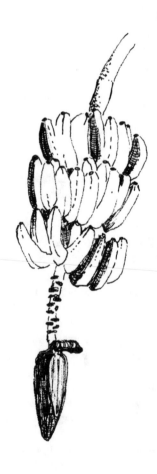

Banana Nut Bread

Yields 1 loaf

This is a good way to utilize bountiful crops of bananas, and is especially good with overripe bananas.

1/2	cup margarine (1 stick)
1	cup sugar
2	eggs
2	teaspoons vanilla
1 1/2	cups mashed, ripe or overripe bananas
2	cups sifted flour
1	teaspoon salt
1/2	teaspoon baking soda
2/3	cup broken nuts

1. Preheat oven to 325° F. Grease a 2-quart loaf pan.
2. In a large mixing bowl, cream margarine, and sugar. Add eggs, vanilla, and bananas. Blend well. Beat in remaining ingredients.
3. Pour into loaf pan. Bake 1 hour and 20 minutes or until toothpick inserted in center comes out clean.
4. Remove from pan while still warm. Cool before slicing.

Cornbread

Yields 1 loaf

This corn bread is moist, sweet, and very filling.

1	cup flour
1	cup wheat germ, plain or honey/brown sugar-coated
1	cup yellow corn meal
1/2	cup sugar
1	teaspoon salt
1	tablespoon plus 2 teaspoons baking powder
1/8	teaspoon nutmeg
3	large eggs or 4 medium, beaten well
1 1/2	cups milk, whole or skim
5	tablespoons melted margarine

1. Preheat oven to 400° F. Grease a 2-quart loaf pan. This has a tendency to stick in the center so be sure the bottom is well greased.
2. Stir all dry ingredients in a large mixing bowl until well blended. Add remaining ingredients. (You don't need a mixer with this recipe; it's quite wet and a spoon will do.) Stir until well blended.
3. Pour into loaf pan, bake (until toothpick inserted in center comes out clean) about 40-45 minutes. Remove from pan while warm.

Fresh Mango Bread

Yields 1 loaf

This recipe comes from a great cook an old and dear friend Clare Gray. She has a huge cookbook collection and taught me that one doesn't necessarily have to cook to enjoy cookbooks. Reading them is wonderful entertainment.

1/2 cup margarine
3/4 cup sugar
2   eggs
2   cups sifted flour
1/4 teaspoon salt
2   teaspoons baking soda
1/2 teaspoon cinnamon
1/8 teaspoon ginger
2/3 cup fresh mango, finely chopped
1   tablespoon lime juice
1   teaspoon vanilla
1/2 cup broken walnuts
1/2 cup raisins (optional)

1. Preheat oven to 350° F.
2. In a large bowl, cream margarine, sugar, and eggs.
3. Sift all dry ingredients together. Blend into above mixture.
4. Stir in mango, lime juice, vanilla, nuts, and raisins.
5. Pour into a well-greased loaf pan. Bake 1 hour or until a toothpick inserted comes out clean. Easier to slice the next day.

Coconut Tea Bread

Yields 1 loaf

2 1/2 cups flour
3/4   cup sugar
1 1/2 teaspoons baking powder
1/2   teaspoon cinnamon
1/8   teaspoon cloves
Whisper of ginger
1/2   teaspoon salt
1   cup shredded coconut
1   cup milk
3   tablespoons melted margarine
1   teaspoon vanilla
1   large egg
1/4   cup tiny pieces fresh coconut (optional)

1. Preheat oven to 350° F.
2. In a large mixing bowl blend flour, sugar, baking powder, cinnamon, cloves, ginger, salt, and shredded coconut. Slowly add milk, margarine, vanilla, and egg. Blend well. Stir in fresh coconut.
3. Pour into well-greased loaf pan. Bake about 45-60 minutes or until toothpick inserted comes out clean.

Cranberry Nut Bread

Yields 1 loaf

1	fresh orange
2	tablespoons butter
1	egg
1	cup sugar
1	cup chopped cranberries
1/2	cup chopped walnuts
2	cups flour
1/2	teaspoon salt
1	teaspoon baking soda

1. Preheat oven to 325° F.
2. Carefully grate the orange rind, only the shiny orange peel. Don't get into the white, it's bitter. Then juice the orange and add enough boiling water to juice, making 3/4 cup liquid. Add butter and rind to this liquid.
3. In a mixing bowl, mix egg and sugar. Blend well.
4. Stir in orange mixture, then cranberries, and walnuts.
5. Sift dry ingredients together. Slowly and gently stir into cranberry mixture or batter will turn black.
6. Pour into greased 9 x 5 inch loaf pan. Bake 1 hour.

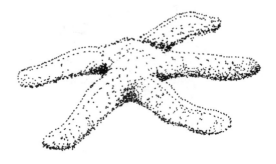

The common starfish possesses the amazing ability to regenerate lost arms.

Barnacle Barb's Avocado Bread

Yields 1 loaf

1/2 cup margarine
3/4 cup sugar
3/4 cup avocado, mashed
2   cups flour
1   teaspoon baking powder
1   teaspoon baking soda
1/4 teaspoon salt
1   teaspoon vanilla
1   teaspoon lime juice
1/3 cup milk
1/2 cup almonds, sliced

1. Preheat oven at 350° F.
2. Cream margarine, add sugar, avocado and eggs, blend well.
3. Sift together dry ingredients.
4. Mix vanilla, lime juice and milk.
5. Alternate liquid and dry ingredients into avocado mixture.
6. Fold in nuts.
7. Grease 9 x 5 x 3 inch loaf pan, pour in batter. Bake 1 hour or until toothpick inserted comes out clean.

Breadfruit

Breadfruit Tea Bread

Yields 1 loaf

This is the famous fruit which caused Captain William Bligh of the H.M.S. Bounty so much grief.

2	eggs
1/3	cup oil
1	cup coconut milk*
1	cup ripe breadfruit, mashed
1 3/4	cups flour
2	teaspoons baking powder
1/2	teaspoon baking soda
1/2	cup light brown sugar
1/2	teaspoon cinnamon
1/4	teaspoon ginger

1. Preheat oven to 325° F.
2. In a large mixing bowl, beat eggs, oil, and coconut milk. Blend in breadfruit until smooth. Add remaining ingredients, and blend well.
3. Pour into well-greased loaf pan. Bake 1 hour or until toothpick inserted comes out clean.

* See coconut milk recipe.

Hops and Barley Bread

Yields 1 loaf

3	cups self-rising flour
3	tablespoons sugar
1	regular size can of beer
1/2	cup sunflower seeds, shelled of course

1. Preheat oven to 400° F.
2. Combine all ingredients, blend well. Pour into well-greased loaf pan.
3. Bake about 30 minutes.

Golfball Coral

Calamondin Bread

Yields 1 loaf

3/4	cup blenderized calamondins (seeds removed)
1/3	cup sugar
1/3	cup margarine
1	egg
3/4	cup brown sugar
1	teaspoon salt
1	teaspoon baking soda
1/4	teaspoon cloves

Whisper of ginger

3/4	teaspoon cinnamon
1 1/3	cups flour
1/2	cup broken pecans

1. Preheat oven to 350° F.
2. Cut calamondins in half. Remove seeds. Whiz calamondins in food processor or blender.
3. Cream together sugar and margarine. Add calamondins, brown sugar, and egg, blend well. Add remaining ingredients. Pour into a greased loaf pan.
4. Bake 30-35 minutes or until toothpick inserted comes out clean. Cuts better the next day.

Speedy Garlic Bread

Yields 1 loaf

1	long loaf French bread
2 or 3	cloves fresh garlic, crushed
1/2	stick margarine or butter

Oregano (optional)
Aluminum foil (optional)

1. Preheat oven to 450° F, unless broiling.
2. Place garlic and butter in a small sauce pan or dish and melt over low heat or in a microwave oven.
3. Slice bread in half lengthwise, and brush both cut sides of bread with butter/garlic mixture. Sprinkle on a bare hint of oregano if desired.
4. If baking, put buttered sides of bread together and wrap in foil, place in oven for 10-15 minutes. If broiling, for a crunchy, toasty bread, place open-faced, butter side up under broiler, watch carefully to prevent burning.
5. Serve immediately.

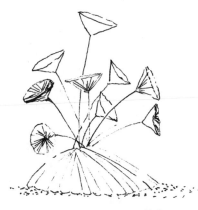

Mermaid's Wineglass (Acetabularia Crenulata) is a light green alga grown in calm waters. The entire wineglass is a single cell and is shown left at actual size.

Saltwater Bread

Yields 1 loaf

This bread recipe was passed from boat to boat by Biscayne Bay Power Squadron members. Small boats don't have ovens so instructions for stove-top baking are included.

1 1/2	cups seawater*
1 1/2	tablespoons sugar
1	tablespoon dried yeast
4-4 1/2	cups flour

1.   Stir sugar and yeast into sea water.
2.   Stir in about 2 cups flour, then remove jewelry, grease hands, and work in remaining 2 cups flour. Dough will be sticky, add enough flour so it becomes manageable, usually about 1/2 cup more. Form into a ball and rub the outside with margarine.
3.   To bake in oven, turn dough into a well-greased 2-quart loaf pan. To bake on top of stove, place dough in a well-greased 4-quart pan with lid, and straight sides. Cover with plastic wrap and place in sun or a warm place to rise, about 2 hours or until double in size. Remove plastic wrap.
4.   Oven baking—bake at 375° F for 35-40 minutes, or until golden. Top of stove—place lid on pan, bake over slow flame or low on electric burner for 30 minutes. Carefully remove half-baked loaf, quickly re-grease pan (I'm extra cautious) and replace loaf in pan upside down. Replace lid and continue baking 30 more minutes.
5.   Remove from pan while warm. Delicious!

*If ocean water is unavailable, health food stores carry sea salt, which is harvested by evaporating sea water. Add 2 1/4 teaspoons salt to 1 1/2 cups tap water to make simulated sea water.

Cuban Bread

Yields 2 loaves

1	package yeast (or 1 tablespoon)
2	cups warm water
1	tablespoon salt
1	tablespoon sugar
7	or more cups flour

1. In a large mixing bowl, blend together salt, yeast, sugar and water.
2. Using an electric mixer, blend in about 1/2 the flour.
3. Remove all jewelry and rub hands with margarine. Knead in remaining flour. When dough is no longer sticky and is soft, warm, and sponge-like in appearance, it is ready. You may have to add a bit more flour, but you'll know.
4. Place dough in a large greased bowl and cover top of bowl with plastic wrap. Place in sun or a warm spot. It takes about 1 hour to double in size.
5. Punch down, (make a fist and push down to bottom of bowl). Knead about 6 times. Divide into 2 pieces and shape into long loaves. Place on greased cookie sheet. Cover with cloth, let rise until double in size.
6. Place in cold oven. Bake at 400° F for about 35 minutes. Bread will be a very pale tan with crunchy crust.
7. Best served warm.

Bran Nut Muffins

Yields 24 muffins

2	cups sour milk* or buttermilk
1/2	cup oil
1/2	cup light brown sugar, firmly packed
1	cup sugar
2	eggs
1	teaspoon vanilla
2 1/2	teaspoons baking soda
1	teaspoon salt
1/2	teaspoon cinnamon
2 1/2	cups sifted flour
2 1/2	cups raisin bran cereal
1/2	cup broken walnuts or pecans

Muffin papers (optional)

1. Preheat oven to 400° F. Line muffin tin with papers or grease tin.
2. In a large mixing bowl combine milk, oil, sugars, eggs, and vanilla. Blend well with electric mixer. Add remaining ingredients. Blend again.

3.   Fill muffin cups almost to the top. Bake 15-20 minutes. This batter will keep several days in the refrigerator.
4.   Serve warm or cold with butter. A great breakfast treat and good snack food on trips.

* Sour milk can be made by mixing 1 3/4 cup whole or skim milk with 1/4 cup vinegar or lime juice.

Sweet Potato Biscuits

Yields about 1 dozen

1   cup flour, sifted
1   tablespoon baking powder
1/2   teaspoon salt
Whisper of ginger
1   tablespoon cane syrup or honey
1/3   cup melted margarine
2   tablespoons milk
1   cup mashed cooked sweet potatoes
1/4   cup water

1.   Preheat oven to 400° F.
2.   Combine dry ingredients in a large bowl. Blend in honey, margarine, milk, and sweet potatoes. Gradually add water.
3.   Place dough on a floured board. Knead until smooth. Roll out to 1/2 inch thick. Cut out with pastry cutter or cut into squares.
4.   Bake for 15-20 minutes or until light brown. Serve hot with butter.

Drop Biscuits

Yields 16 biscuits

2   cups flour
3 1/2   teaspoons baking powder
1   teaspoon salt
1/3   cup oil
2/3   cup milk

1.   Preheat oven to 475° F.
2.   Measure dry ingredients into a bowl. Pour oil and milk into a cup, but do not stir. Pour all at once into the bowl. Stir with a fork until the dough cleans the side of the bowl and forms a ball.
3.   Drop from a spoon onto an ungreased cookie sheet. Bake 10-12 minutes or until brown.

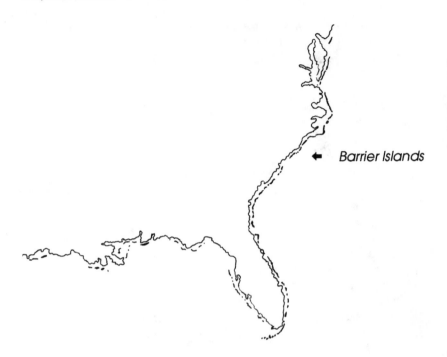

Barrier Islands

Beaches

People have always been and always will be captivated by beaches. It's interesting that a beach can be so restless yet so tranquil.

Have you ever considered how it all works? Beaches, always in motion, are formed by the combination of wind, sand, and water. Waves transport sand suspended in water from offshore sandbars to the swash, the area at water's edge where waves break. Wind then picks it up and moves it inland. As sand accumulates above the tide line, grasses spring up and capture the blowing sand, anchoring it with extensive root systems and forming dunes.

This area, called the pioneer zone, is dominated by hardy grasses and vines, such as sea oats and railroad vine. Salt spray plays a key role in this plant community by selectively killing off alien plants which are intolerant to high salinity.

As these pioneer plants flourish and sand dunes build up, the soil becomes somewhat fertile and less salty—suitable for woody or herbaceous plants, like seagrape and sea lavender. With this natural change, the pioneer zone becomes the scrub zone, which when completely stabilized, evolves into the forest zone, consisting of pineland or hammock trees and plants. These three zones are collectively known as the coastal strand.

East coast beaches are usually located on offshore barrier islands, which run almost the entire length of the Atlantic and Gulf coasts, shielding the continental United States from direct contact with the sea. These ever-changing slivers of sand, constantly buffeted by wind and sea, host one of the most fragile ecosystems in our environment. Between these islands and undeveloped areas of the mainland lie salt marshes and mangrove nurseries, some of the most naturally productive areas of the world.

Beaches are enriched by a unique sand transport system. Waves that roll straight onto the beach deposit sand directly ahead of them. Waves that hit the beach at an angle are influenced by "longshore drift," the same motion that keeps a bather from staying in line with his beach blanket. This current moves the sand up and down the beach, eroding one area and nourishing another.

Despite man's efforts to develop and preserve the coastline, nature has its own ways of protecting the beaches. Dunes are a good example. Vast storehouses of sand which, if left undisturbed, help prevent beach erosion. Dunes can be demolished when great storm waves pull sand back into the sea. As a result, breaking waves lose their intensity as they roll through shallower water. While this sand, once again under the influence of the longshore drift, might not end up exactly where it came from, it will eventually return to shore.

Beaches are born of motion and react to dynamic forces, as they were intended to do, by changing shape naturally.

Coquina Chowder

Serves 2

This isn't a serious food, but children love the "hunt." Coquinas are tiny clams with 1/2-inch-long pastel-colored shells, found in the swash on Florida's west coast beaches. The swash is the section of beach where waves break. Standing there wiggling your toes as waves recede, you will see hundreds of these rainbow-hued clams trying to burrow under the sand. Scoop them into a colander to wash away the sand.

2	pints coquinas
1	cup finely potatoes, chopped
2-3	tablespoons margarine
1/2	cup onion, chopped
1/2	cup fresh mushrooms, sliced
1/2	teaspoon parsley
1 1/2	cups milk

Salt and pepper to taste

1. Wash coquinas in fresh water. Put into pan and cover with water. Bring to a boil, simmer 20 minutes. Strain out shells. Put potatoes into broth and cook until potatoes are done.
2. Sauté onions and mushrooms in margarine until done. Add to coquina and potatoes. Add remaining ingredients. Bring to a simmer. Serve immediately.

Sea Lettuce Soup

Serves 4

This is only for adventuresome souls. Sea lettuce or ulva can be found clinging to rocks on the flats. It's bright green, somewhat translucent, and looks similar to lettuce.

1-2 tablespoons margarine
1/2 cup onion, chopped
1/2 cup celery, chopped
1 cup cooked chicken, cut into tiny pieces
1/2 cup ulva, cut up*
1/2 cup carrots, sliced (rounds)
1 tablespoon soy sauce
1/2 teaspoon black pepper
3 cups water

In a medium sauce pan, sauté margarine, onions, and celery. Add remaining ingredients. Simmer 20 minutes.

*Note: Wash and clean ulva in fresh water. Keep your eyes peeled for sea life clinging to the blades.

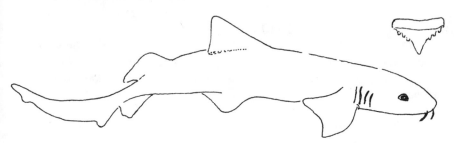

The Nurse Shark is six to fourteen feet long, with tan coloring.

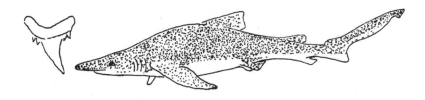

The Sand Shark is three to ten feet long, gray-brown, with a light underbelly.

The Hammerhead Shark grows to twenty feet, is tan with a light underbelly, and has eyes that move independently.

The Black Tip Shark is two to six feet long and gray with a light underbelly.

Black Tip Chowder

Serves 4

1	cup potatoes, chopped (peeling optional)
1	cup carrots, chopped
3	or more tablespoons margarine
1/2	cup onion, chopped
1/2	cup celery, chopped
1 1/2	pounds lean, mild fish, cut into bite size pieces (young black-tip shark is good)
1/4	teaspoon Beau Monde Seasoning
1-2	teaspoons Worcestershire sauce
2 1/2-3	cups whole or skim milk

Salt and pepper to taste

1.   In a 2-quart pot, simmer potatoes and carrots in a small amount of water until done, but firm.
2.   Sauté celery in margarine until soft, then add onions and fish, continue cooking until done, but not brown.
3.   Add this mixture to the vegetables. Blend in all remaining ingredients. Heat to just below boiling. Cook about 10-15 minutes. Serve hot.

Lobster Bisque

Yields 6-8 servings (9 cups)

6	cups strained chicken broth (canned or homemade—see following recipe on page 46)
2	cups cooked lobster, finely chopped (about 1 1/2 pounds)
1	cup Half and Half
5	tablespoons cornstarch

White pepper to taste

1.   Put broth into large kettle, add lobster, pepper, and Half and Half. Heat until very warm, but not boiling.
2.   Dissolve cornstarch in 1/2-2/3 cup water, add to bisque stirring constantly until bisque boils. Lower heat and continue stirring so it will not stick to bottom of pan. Simmer at least one hour to enhance lobster flavor. Serve hot.

Homemade Chicken Broth

Yields 6 cups

1   chicken (1 1/2-2 pounds)
2   tablespoons salt
1   cup carrots, sliced
1   cup celery,sliced
2   teaspoons dried parsley

1.   In a large pot, cover chicken with water, bring to a boil. Pour chicken into colandar, rinse bird. Discard water, wash residue off sides of pot.
2.   Put chicken back into pot, barely cover with water (about 8 cups), boil. Add vegetables and seasonings. Simmer one hour.

Conch Chowder

Serves 8-10

This is a fun recipe—anything goes. All measurements are approximate. Deletions or deviations (except the conch of course) can be delicious, so be creative. Leftovers or whatever you may have in your refrigerator which hasn't been set aside for the dog, should be thrown in. Good luck!

2   medium onions, chopped
1   large green pepper, chopped
2   stalks or ribs celery, chopped
2   cloves garlic, crushed
1/4 cup margarine (1/2 stick)
8   large conchs, blenderized
16   ounce can tomatoes with water
15   ounce can black beans (optional, but gives nice color)
2   cans sliced potatoes, drained, or 4 large fresh, diced
1   box frozen mixed vegetables
2   tablespoons parsley
Pickapeppa or any steak sauce to taste
5   bay leaves
3   chicken bouillon cubes
2   teaspoons oregano
Tabasco sauce to taste
1   quart V-8 juice

1.   In your largest pot with lid, sauté onion, garlic, green pepper, and celery in margarine until soft. Add remaining ingredients. Bring to a boil, reduce heat. Cover and simmer about 2 hours.
2.   Serve with homemade bread and beer.

Garbanzo Bean Soup

Serves 4

4	strips bacon, chopped
1/2	cup onion, chopped
1	can garbanzo beans
2	large potatoes, chopped into bite-size pieces
2	bouillon cubes—your choice
1	tablespoon Worcestershire sauce

Salt and pepper to taste

1. Sauté onion and bacon until golden.
2. Pour garbanzos (including water) into large pot, add 2 cups water. Add potatoes, bring to a boil, then reduce to a simmer to cook potatoes. Add bouillon cubes.
3. When potatoes are cooked, remove 1 cup of this mixture and blenderize until smooth. Pour back into pot. This thickens the mixture.
4. Add onion, bacon, Worcestershire sauce and season to taste. Simmer another 30 minutes to blend flavors.

Asparagus Soup

Serves 4

1	can asparagus (approximately 15 ounces)
2	cups fresh mushrooms, sliced
1/4	cup onions, chopped
4	tablespoons margarine

Liquid from asparagus plus enough water to make 1 1/2 cups

3	chicken bouillon cubes
1 1/2	cups milk

Pepper to taste

1. Cut large mushroom slices into bite-size pieces.
2. Sauté onions and mushrooms in margarine until soft.
3. Pour asparagus/water liquid into above mixture, heat just below boiling and add bouillon cubes. Stir until melted.
4. On a dinner plate, mash asparagus with a fork—all except tips, add to liquid. Then add milk, heat, but do not boil. Cook about 10 minutes. Pepper to taste. Serve hot.

Eastern Brown Pelican (protected)

Catch of the Day
and Other Entrées

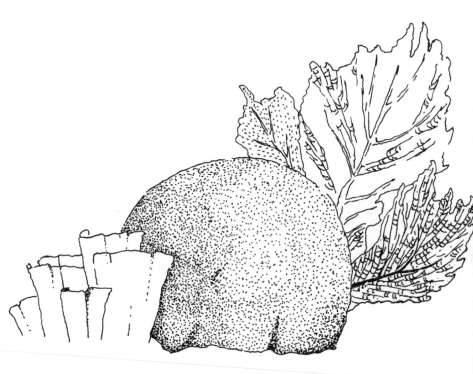

Fire Coral   *Smooth Starlet Coral*   *Sea Fan*

The Coral Reef

For anyone who has been diving, the words "coral reef" bring images of the basic coral foundation, along with the entire, complex marine community that dwells there.

The neophyte diver is almost overwhelmed by the abundant marine life associated with a healthy reef. Fish of every size, shape, and brilliant color—some shimmering with iridescence, others dark and velvety—glide gracefully among the magnificent coral formations. Lavender-hued soft corals and richly colored sponges sway in the current. Twinkling eyes peek from every shadowy nook and cranny. Reef music—tinkling, bubbling, murmuring, snapping sounds—fills your ears. This is not a silent world. In every direction is a myriad of life, so in tune with itself that the diver feels awkward and ungainly. No doubt, you are the intruder, the alien in this spectacular fluid world.

It all starts with the lower animal—the reef itself. Most reef-building corals are colonial. These soft-bodied animals, called polyps, reproduce by dividing off the original polyp. The new animals, in turn, multiply until the colony forms the branching, massive shapes we think of as coral.

They also reproduce sexually; sperm are released into the water, entering another polyp to fertilize the eggs within. The embryos are then released into the water as larvae, called planulae, which are carried by currents, until they find an appropriate place to settle. Having selected its permanent home, a planula comes to rest on the bottom and secretes a calcareous skeleton which binds it to that place forever, and a new coral colony begins.

Coral is very limited in where it can live. Bright sunlight and warm, clear water with the proper salinity, nutrient and oxygen content determine the very select environment in which coral thrives. Coral's tiny tentacles wave swimming organisms into its mouth and sweep away sediment that would clog and smother it.

In addition to providing a habitat for sea life, the slow growing coral is also food for creatures such as parrotfish and starfish. Balance is so delicate between growth and this natural predation that an environmental upset can easily tip the scales onto an irreversible destructive path. Environmental changes, such as dredging or extreme weather conditions, can alter currents and sedimentation patterns, and toll the death knell for a reef and all its dwellers. The reef will continue to flourish as long as the conditions that originally induced coral growth are fulfilled.

There are two separate populations on reefs—diurnal or daytime feeders, and nocturnal or nighttime feeders. Those residents who have been busy foraging all day will go to their individual retreats to take shelter and sleep. Nocturnal reef dwellers then emerge to begin their active period. If you are fortunate enough to do both a day and a night dive, you could see two different groups of residents on the same reef. The reef supports twice as much life with this incredible 'round-the-clock system of resource sharing.

Florida's John Pennecamp Coral Reef State Park, the only one of its kind in the continental United States, has about forty different types of coral. It's not necessary to dive to great depths to see the wonder of this treasure. At low tide, the reef is actually awash in some places.

Remember to look, not touch. Coral and sponges can sting, and handling kills the coral.

For those who cannot snorkle, the glass-bottom boat out of John Pennekamp is the next best thing to being down under. Sunny, calm mornings are best—the colors are richest then.

Once you have seen the breathtaking beauty of the reef, you will understand why its safety and continued survival cause such a furor among the informed. Future generations have the right to enjoy this natural wonder.

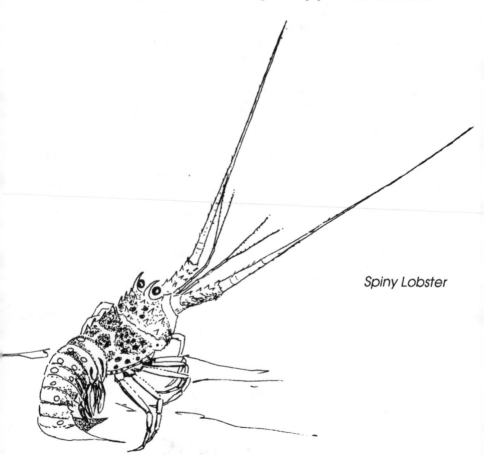

Spiny Lobster

Broiled Florida Lobster

Ask for "Green Lobster" at the seafood market. These are uncooked.

Enough tails to feed your crew—1 tail per person plus a couple extra (purchase six tails for 4 people)
Butter or margarine for dunking—2 tablespoons per person
Lime wedges—1/2 lime per person

1. Split tails lengthwise, remove vein. Lay lobster in a shallow pan.
2. Lay shell side up, broil 5 minutes. Turn over, spread on a little margarine, place under broiler—about 5 more minutes or until meat is firm and white and no longer translucent.
3. Serve with melted butter and lime wedges.

Grilled Lobster

Follow instructions for amount and initial preparations as for Broiled Lobster.

Cook outside over charcoal or gas grill fire. Lay split tails shell side up—over medium heat. Cook about 10 minutes or until done with lid down. Serve at once with melted butter and lime wedges.

Sizzle and Squeak
(Lobster Tails)

Serves 4

6   spiny lobster tails, split and deveined
2-3 cloves garlic, crushed
1   teaspoon salt
Pepper to taste
2   tablespoons parsley, finely chopped
2/3 cup margarine, melted
1/4 cup lime juice

Combine garlic, salt, pepper, parsley, margarine, and lime juice. Brush on lobster. Place shell side up in shallow baking pan. Broil 5 minutes. Remove from heat. Flip lobsters over. Spoon on remaining margarine mixture. Return to broiler for 5 minutes or until done. Watch. You want them to sizzle and squeak, but not burn! Serve immediately.

Lobster Enchilada

Serves 4

4   spiny lobster tails*, shelled and deveined, cut into chunks
16 ounce can whole tomatoes
2   cloves garlic, crushed
1   cup green pepper, chopped
1   cup onion, chopped
Olive oil
Salt and pepper to taste
1/2 teaspoon Beau Monde seasoning
2   bay leaves
1/4 teaspoon oregano
1/4 teaspoon ground cumin
2   Key limes

Put onion, green pepper, garlic, and olive oil into a large skillet and sauté until vegetables are limp. Add remaining ingredients except lobster. Cover. Simmer 20 minutes. Stir in lobster. Cover. Cook an additional 10 minutes. Serve over rice.

*2 pounds rock shrimp may be substituted for lobster

Butter Fried Lobster

Serves 4

3-4 tablespoons butter
3-4 tablespoons margarine
4-6 spiny lobster tails, shelled, deveined, cut up
Whisper of salt
Juice of 1/2 lime

1.   Melt butter and margarine in a heavy skillet until hot but not sizzling. Lay in lobster meat. Cover. Cook on low heat 5 minutes.
2.   Remove cover. Add lime juice and salt. Increase heat until butter is sizzling. Brown lobster. Serve immediately.

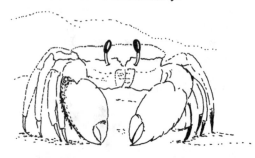

Ghost Crab

Crab Cakes

Serves 4

1　egg, beaten until foamy
2　tablespoons mayonnaise
1/2　teaspoon dry mustard
1/4　bird pepper, finely chopped (optional) or pepper to taste
1/2　teaspoon salt
1　tablespoon parsley
1/3　cup bread crumbs
1　pound crab claw meat
Margarine
Oil
Lime wedges

1.　Combine egg, mayonnaise, dry mustard, pepper, and salt. Blend well. Fold in crab, parsley, and bread crumbs.
2.　Divide crab into 8 portions. Shape into ovals about a half inch thick. Chill one hour.
3.　Heat oil and margarine in a large skillet until just sizzling. Fry crab until golden and crisp. Drain on paper towels. Serve with lime wedges.

Pineapple Crab

Serves 4

1　pound lump crab
1/4　cup mayonnaise
1　teaspoon pimento, chopped
1/2　teaspoon salt
3/4　teaspoon Worcestershire sauce
4　dashes Tabasco
4　large pineapple slices
1　cup crushed Rice Krispies (pour into a baggie, crush with hands)

1.　Preheat oven to 350° F.
2.　Mix crab, mayonnaise, pimento, salt, Worcestershire, and Tabasco. Blend well.
3.　Coat pineapple slices with Rice Krispies. Lay in a buttered baking dish. Top each pineapple with crab mixture. Top with remaining Rice Krispies.
4.　Bake 20-30 minutes or until hot. Serve immediately.

Key Lime Fish

Serves 4

1 1/2-2	pounds fresh grouper fillets
2	tablespoons butter, melted
1/4	cup lime juice
1	teaspoon tarragon
1/4	cup onion, diced

Salt and pepper

1. Preheat oven to 325° F.
2. In a shallow oven-proof dish place fillets in a single layer. Sprinkle on lime juice. Drizzle on butter. Add onions, tarragon, salt, and pepper. Cover with foil.
3. Bake for 15-20 minutes or until done. Serve immediately.

Snapper Piccata

Serves 4

2	pounds snapper fillets

Salt and pepper

Flour

3	tablespoons butter
1	tablespoon olive oil
2	cloves garlic, crushed
1 1/2	cups mushrooms, sliced
1	lemon
2	tablespoons capers with juice
1/2-3/4	cup white wine

Hog Fish

1. Sprinkle fish with salt and pepper. Coat with flour.
2. Combine butter and olive oil in a large skillet. Sauté fish until done—about 10 minutes depending on thickness. Remove and keep warm.
3. Add mushrooms and garlic to skillet. Sauté in drippings until mushrooms are somewhat limp. Return fish to pan. Add juice from 1/2 lemon, capers with juice and wine. Cover and simmer 5 minutes. Serve over wild rice.

Flying Fish Bajan Style

Serves 4

This is not standard fare in the United States, but it is a local favorite in Barbados. The only place I know to get flying fish is a bait store. Make sure it's fresh.

8   fillets (8 fish filleted in a butterfly fashion)
1   small onion, grated
1   large clove garlic, crushed
Jane's Krazy Mixed Up Salt
Pepper to taste
1   teaspoon lime juice
1   egg, beaten
Cracker meal
Oil and margarine
Lime wedges

Rock Beauty

1.   Combine onion, garlic, Krazy salt, pepper, and lime juice. Lightly coat fish. Refrigerate 1 hour.
2.   Roll fillets in egg, then cracker meal. Sauté in an oil and margarine combination. Serve immediately with lime wedges.

Sautéed Fish

Serves 4

Fish fillets—enough to feed your crew, about 1/3-1/2 pound per person or 2 pounds for service of 4
1/3   cup flour
1/3   cornmeal
Lawry's Seasoned Salt and pepper to taste
Margarine
Oil
Lime wedges or sauces (optional)

1.   Rinse and dry fillets. Use your favorite. I prefer snapper, grouper, or dolphin.
2.   On a piece of waxed paper, mix flour and cornmeal in equal parts.
3.   Heat margarine and oil over medium heat. I use equal parts. The oil seems to keep the margarine from burning. Oil/margarine mix should be about 1/8 inch deep in skillet. You may have to add more as you fry.
4.   Sprinkle salt and pepper on fillets. Roll in flour mixture. Cook over medium heat until golden on both sides, about 5 minutes each side, depending on thickness. Lay on paper towel to drain.
5.   Serve at once, lime wedges and sauces optional. See Cocktail Sauce recipe.

Fish Fillets Amandine

1/4-1/2 cup almonds, sliced
1-2   teaspoons parsley, chopped
Lime wedges

1. Prepare sautéed fish recipe.
2. Sauté sliced almonds in margarine until brown. Sprinkle almonds over fish.
3. Garnish with chopped parsley.
4. Serve at once with lime wedges.

Checkered Puffer

Campfire Fish

Serves 4-6

This is my version of an old recipe for cooking fish over an open fire. The original recipe came from an old fishing camp on the lower Florida Keys.

1/4 cup margarine, melted (1/2 stick)
1/3 cup firmly packed light brown sugar
1/3 cup fresh lime juice
3   tablespoons soy sauce
Dash of Wrights liquid smoke
2-3 pounds fresh fish fillets, snapper, grouper, or dolphin
Broiler foil

1. Combine first 5 ingredients in a small bowl, stir until sugar is dissolved. Yield about 1 cup.
2. Place fish in a plastic bag, pour marinade over, squeeze out excess air and seal. Marinate 1-2 hours, turning once or twice during process to redistribute liquid. Place bag in a bowl as a precaution against leaks. Refrigerate.
3. Fashion a shallow pan out of aluminum foil, large enough to hold fish in a single layer. A grill basket can also be used.
4. On an outdoor grill, lay fish in "foil pan," pour marinade over, cook over a low fire, turning fish once during process. Baste frequently with marinade. Cooks in about 20 minutes. Serve at once.

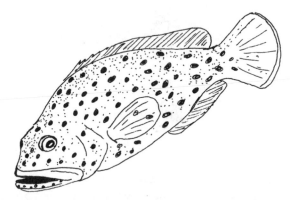

The Redhind Grouper is pink with red dots and is excellent to eat.

Cayman Islands Fish

In Grand Cayman, fishing guides delight visitors by serving this simple but elegant fare over an open fire on the beach after diving all day.

Fish fillets, your favorite kind, enough to feed your crew, about 1/3-1/2 pound per person (snapper, grouper, or dolphin is best).

Onions, thin sliced
Margarine
Limes & Tabasco sauce
Pickapeppa Sauce
Salt and pepper
Heavy duty broiler foil

1. Tear off a generous piece of foil, enough to envelop the fish with a good seal.
2. Lay fillets in a single layer, on foil. Sprinkle on salt, pepper, Pickapeppa, Tabasco. Squeeze on lime juice. Top each fillet with onion slice and a pat of margarine. Seal foil with a double fold.
3. Bake over charcoal grill, wood fire (on rack), or in 325° F oven for about 30 minutes, or until done. Serve at once with lime wedges.

Grill Basket

Bacon Wrapped Fish

1 inch thick fish fillets, enough to feed your crew, 1/3-1/2 pounds per person (grouper will do nicely)
Bacon slices
Pam spray
Grill basket—This is one of those handy items constructed of two wire racks which hinge together at the back and cooks delicate foods over an open fire.

1.   Spray grill basket with Pam
2.   Lay raw bacon in one side of grill basket. Top with fish. Cover fish with final layer of bacon.
3.   Cook over barbecue grill or open campfire on the beach until bacon is crispy and brown, about 10 minutes each side depending on the thickness of the fish. Serve immediately.

CAUTION! Do not wander away and leave this unattended, or you will wander back to a cinder in a basket. Bacon grease tends to make the grill flare.

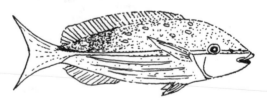

Crispy Broiled Yellowtail

Serves 4

4	yellowtail, sans heads, cleaned, scaled
1/2	cup olive oil
1/2	teaspoon salt
1/8	teaspoon black pepper
1/8	teaspoon red pepper
1/8	teaspoon ginger
1/8	teaspoon cloves
1/8	teaspoon dry mustard
Whisper of cardamom	
1 1/2	teaspoons paprika
Key limes, wedges	

Score yellowtail. Combine olive oil and seasonings. Place fish on broiler pan, brush with oil mixture. Broil close to heat source. Flip fish, brush, broil—about 10-15 minutes depending on size of fish. Serve with lime wedges.

Shrimp Basics

Serves 2

1 pound headless shrimp
1 quart water
1 teaspoon sugar
1 teaspoon vinegar
2 teaspoons salt

Shrimp cleaning tool

Instructions for raw shrimp
1. In a large pot, combine all ingredients except shrimp. Cover. Bring to a boil.
2. To prepare raw shrimp, clean prior to cooking using a special shrimp cleaning tool. Shrimp are shelled and deveined in one motion, time is cut considerably. They are available at any store, but especially seafood markets. People in seafood shops can show you how to use them. There are also instructions on the handle. With experience it can take as little as 10 minutes to clean 1 pound of shrimp.
3. Drop cleaned shrimp into boiling water and watch. By the time the water begins to boil, the shrimp have turned pink and are done—about 3 minutes. Pour into colander, rinse with cold water. Chill.

Dilly Shrimp

Serves 4

1 1/2 pounds shrimp, shelled and deveined
2 tablespoons onion, finely chopped
4 tablespoons margarine
2 tablespoons flour
1 cup milk
1/4 cup dry white wine
1 tablespoon dill
Salt and pepper

Melt margarine in a large skillet, add onion. Sauté until limp. Stir in flour, slowly add milk, stirring constantly to prevent lumping. Cook over medium heat, stirring constantly until thickened. Add remaining ingredients. Simmer 5-10 minutes or until shrimp are done.

Sea Fan, a living animal

Tomato Shrimp Curry

Serves 4

1 1/2	pounds shrimp, shelled and deveined
1	cup onion, chopped
1	clove garlic, crushed
Oil	
1	cup fresh tomatoes, chopped
1	teaspoon lime juice
1	hot chili pepper, chopped
2	teaspoons curry powder
1/4	teaspoon ginger
1/8	teaspoon turmeric
1/2	cup water

Using a large covered skillet, sauté onion and garlic in a small amount of oil until soft. Add all remaining ingredients except shrimp. Bring to a boil. Reduce heat, cover. Simmer 15 minutes. Stir in shrimp. Cook additional 10 minutes. Serve over rice.

Pecan Shrimp

Serves 4

1   pound large shrimp, shelled and deveined
1   cup Ritz cracker crumbs
1   cup pecans, finely chopped
1   teaspoon Worcestershire sauce
1/4 cup (4 tablespoons) melted margarine
1   egg

1. Preheat oven to 350° F.
2. Butterfly shrimp and lay flat in a greased baking dish.
3. Whiz crackers and pecans separately in a food processor or blender to make 1 cup each. This can also be done with a rolling pin. Blend into remaining ingredients.
4. Lay pecan mixture, about 1 tablespoon, on each shrimp. Pack firmly into place.
5. Bake for 15 minutes. Serve plain or with garlic butter sauce.

Shrimp Perlo

Serves 4

1 1/2 pounds shrimp, shelled and deveined
3   slices bacon, diced
1   cup green pepper, chopped
1   clove garlic, crushed
1/2 cup onion, chopped
16 ounce can tomatoes with water
1   cup water
1/2 cup uncooked rice, well washed
1   teaspoon salt
1/4 teaspoon pepper
1/4 teaspoon thyme
5-6 dashes Tabasco
2   teaspoons Worcestershire sauce

Using a large covered skillet, fry bacon until crisp. Remove bacon. Sauté peppers, garlic, and onions in bacon fat until limp. Add tomatoes and water. Bring to a boil, stir in rice and seasonings. Cover. Reduce heat to low. Simmer 20 minutes. Add shrimp, cover, cook an additional 10 minutes. Serve immediately.

Shrimp Creole

Serves 4

1 1/2	pounds shrimp, shelled and deveined
1/4	cup flour
1/3	cup oil
1	cup hot water
8	ounce can tomato sauce
1/2	cup onion
1/2	cup parsley
1/4	cup green pepper, chopped
4	cloves garlic, crushed
1 1/2	teaspoons salt
1/2	teaspoon thyme
1/8	teaspoon cayenne pepper
2	whole bay leaves
1	slice lemon
2	cups cooked rice, hot—see Rice Basics recipe

1. In a large covered skillet, blend flour into oil and cook until brown. Slowly add water, stirring constantly until smooth. Add remaining ingredients except rice. Cover. Simmer on low heat 20 minutes.
2. Serve over hot rice.

Puff Fried Shrimp

Serves 6

Simple but real gourmet fare. You'll never eat frozen breaded shrimp again.

2	pounds fresh raw shrimp, without heads (25-30 count* if possible)
1	clove garlic, crushed
1 1/2	cups flour
1	tablespoon baking powder
1/2	teaspoon salt
1/2	cup oil
1	cup water
4	cups oil for deep frying

1. Shell and devein shrimp. See Shrimp Basics recipe, for cleaning instructions. Leaving tails on is optional. Dry and lay on paper towels. Rub with garlic.

2.   Combine all dry ingredients in a small bowl. Blend well. Add oil and stir into a dough-like ball. Sides of bowl will be clean. Slowly stir in water, mixture will have a cake-batter-like consistency.

3.   Pour oil into a small sauce pan or deep fryer. Use enough oil to suspend shrimp during cooking. Heat oil to 375° F or drop a bit of batter in hot oil. It will puff up and rise to the surface immediately when oil is hot enough.

4.   Dip shrimp in batter and fry about 4 at a time for approximately 1 to 2 minutes. Do not over cook, shrimp will be tough. This batter does not get golden brown, but is a light tan when done. Sample a shrimp to get familiar with frying time.

5.   Lay fried shrimp on a cookie sheet lined with paper towels to drain off excess oil. Keep cookie sheet in a warm oven with door open so shrimp will stay crisp and warm until you're done frying.

6.   Serve at once. You do not need sauce with these shrimp. But if you insist, see Cocktail Sauce recipe.

*"Count" means the number of shrimp to the pound. Shrimp with "heads on" results in about 50% waste. Shrimp without heads results in about 10% waste.

Simple Shrimp Scampi

Serves 4

2   pounds medium-large shrimp, shelled, deveined, with tails on
1/3 cup melted margarine
Juice of 3 small Key limes or 2 Persian limes
4   cloves garlic, crushed
1   teaspoon oregano
Parsley

1.   Preheat oven to 350° F.

2.   Find a large flat baking dish as shrimp will be laid out in a single layer. Put margarine in dish and place in hot oven to melt.

3.   Add all remaining ingredients to melted margarine (except shrimp), and stir in.

4.   Lay out shrimp, single layer. Halfway through baking, turn the shrimp over with a spatula.

5.   Bake about 10-15 minutes. Shrimp cook very quickly. They are done as soon as they look pink and soft white, rather than translucent. Serve immediately.

Note: Because of the lime juice and garlic, I omit salt. Place a shaker on the table for those who like salted food.

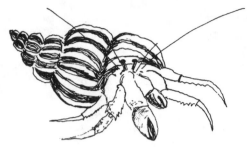

Hermit Crab

Basic Crêpes

Yields about 12-16 five-inch crêpes

Prepare for Seafood Crêpe Recipe

1	cup flour
3	eggs
4	tablespoons oil
1/4	teaspoon salt
1 3/4	cups milk

Butter for frying crêpes

1. Using a small bowl combine all ingredients and only 1/2 cup milk. Blend well by hand until batter is smooth. If you use an electric mixer, use the lowest speed. Too much air beaten into the eggs will cause "holey" crêpes. When the batter is smooth, mix in the remaining milk. For thinner crêpes use more milk. For thicker crêpes use less.

2. Let batter rest 1/2 hour to thicken.

3. In small omelet or crêpe pan melt about 1/2 teaspoon butter over medium-high heat. Pour in a small amount of batter, tip pan to spread around. When the crêpe is *set* on top, flip it over. They are only supposed to be slightly brown. The first two or three might stick. Feed these to the dog and carry on. The pan is simply becoming "seasoned." Stack crêpes on top of each other on a cake rack. Batter keeps for a week refrigerated.

Coral Crab

*Common Atlantic
Vase Snail*

Seafood Crêpes

Prepare Basic Crêpes recipe
1/4 cup butter
1/4 cup onions, minced
1/2 pound lump backfin crab meat
1/2 pound shrimp, shelled and deveined
Salt and pepper to taste
Dash garlic powder
1/4 cup Vermouth

In a large skillet gently sauté butter, seafood, and onions. Season with salt and pepper and garlic. Pour in Vermouth and boil until liquid is almost gone. Pour into bowl and set aside.

Sauce
1/3   cup Vermouth
2   tablespoons cornstarch
2   tablespoons milk
1   pint heavy whipping cream
Salt and pepper to taste
1 1/2   cups grated Swiss cheese
Butter

1. Pour Vermouth into skillet. Boil until about 1 tablespoon is left. Remove from heat. In a small bowl slowly blend cornstarch into milk, stirring so it won't lump. Pour into skillet, blend. Return skillet to low heat. Slowly add cream, salt, and pepper. Stirring constantly, cook until it begins to thicken. Then add 1 cup Swiss cheese. Cook until melted, blending well. Blend 1/2 sauce into seafood mixture.
2. Preheat oven to 400° F.
3. Fill each crêpe with seafood. Roll closed. Place in a buttered oven-proof dish. Spoon remaining sauce over each crêpe. Top with cheese.
4. Bake 15-20 minutes or until bubbly.

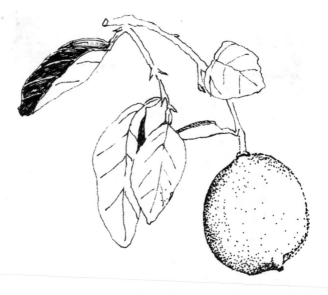

Key Lime

Key Lime *(Citrus aurantifolia)*

Dr. Henry Perrine is credited with introducing limes to Florida when he settled his family on Indian Key in 1838. Wishing to establish a tropical botanical nursery in the lower Florida wilds, Perrine seized every opportunity to spread useful, hardy, exotic plants throughout the uninhabited region.

The existence of naturalized lime trees scattered along the Keys at the turn of the century has been attributed to Dr. Perrine's diligent labor. Locally known as "sours" and "dillies," Key limes and sugary sweet sapodillas were staple fruits of the Florida settler by the early 1900s.

So rugged is the rocky habitat of the Key lime it has been said that the only tools necessary to work a lime grove are muscle, machete, and dynamite! Charlotte and Russell Niedhauk, who tended lime groves on Elliott Key in the 1930s, occasionally imported labor from the mainland. They specified only one job requirement, a pair of good, strong work shoes.

If Key limes are indifferent to soil, they are particular about climate. Growing only on the extreme southern tip of Florida, they require year-round warmth to survive.

The trees mature in three years, producing a small, round exceptionally fragrant, thin-skinned fruit which turns yellow when ripe. The pulp is a uniform pale green color, and rumor has it that the Key lime yields more juice for its volume than any other citrus fruit.

By 1913, the Key lime industry was beginning to emerge. Key lime trees produced a bountiful crop that did not spoil or bruise easily during shipping. In 1923, Key lime production reached its peak and prospered until the hurricane of 1926 dealt the industry a blow from which it never recovered. The last lime packing shed, on Key Largo, stood until its collapse in the 1970s.

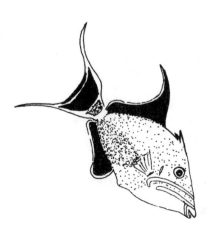

Though not grown commercially today, Key limes are cultivated and enjoyed by the majority of south Florida home owners. When out exploring Keys, hammocks, or uninhabited islands, occasionally one stumbles upon an old homestead, long abandoned. The only signs that these places were once homes are remnants of old water cisterns and a few hardy exotic trees. The old homesteaders' beloved sours and dillies are still struggling to survive against the encroaching tropical undergrowth, and bearing fruit.

Queen Trigger Fish

Lime Marinated Chicken

Serves 4-6

6-8 pieces chicken (skinned if desired)
1/2 cup fresh lime juice
1/4 cup oil
1/4 cup honey
1   garlic clove, crushed
2   tablespoons soy sauce
1/4 teaspoon ground ginger

1. Starting with lime juice, combine all ingredients, stir until well blended.
2. Place chicken in a plastic bag, pour marinade over. Squeeze out excess air, seal. Marinate 3 hours, turning once or twice during process to redistribute liquid. Place bag in bowl as a precaution against leaks. Refrigerate.
3. Cook on barbecue grill, over medium heat about 40 minutes or until done. Serve at once.

Snap Cackle and Pop
(Oven Fried Chicken)

Jo Garvin's lovely country kitchen is complete with a fireplace large enough to accommodate several people standing. Located in Valley Forge, the farmhouse was built in 1731 and was George Washington's Paymaster station during the Revolutionary War. This is one of her creations.

Chicken pieces—legs, wings, thighs, breasts, enough to feed your crew

Margarine
1 large box Rice Krispies
Salt and pepper to taste
Aluminum foil (optional)

1. Preheat oven to 350° F. Crush Rice Krispies in a bowl with your hands, or in a bag, with a rolling pin. One cup will probably coat 4 pieces of chicken.
2. Melt margarine over low heat, start out with one stick, it depends on how much you are making.
3. Wash and pat chicken dry.
4. Covering a cookie sheet or large flat pan with foil is optional, but saves clean-up time later.
5. Dip chicken pieces into the melted margarine, then roll in crushed Krispies. Lay on foil.
6. Bake one hour or until done. Serve hot.

7. This chicken may be prepared for cooking a day ahead. Remove from refrigerator and let sit at room temperature 1 hour before baking. Left over Krispies and margarine may be stored in the refrigerator for future use.

Boiled and Broiled Chicken

Serves 4-6

1 whole chicken
1 onion
1 rib or stalk of celery
Parsley
Salt and pepper

1. Rinse chicken and place in Dutch oven or large pot with lid. Add enough water to cover 2/3 of bird. Toss in vegetables and seasonings, bring to a gentle boil. Cover. Reduce heat, cook about one hour, turning chicken once or twice to cook evenly.
2. When bird is done, test for tenderness with fork, remove from broth. When cool enough to handle, cut in half lengthwise and place skin side up on broiler pan. Sprinkle with salt and pepper. Move oven rack as far from heat source as possible. Place chicken under broiler for about 10-20 minutes. Watch closely, skin will become golden and crispy while meat remains moist and succulent. Serve immediately.

Grilled Chicken

Make above recipe but cook on barbecue grill for a smoky flavor, instead of under broiler. This chicken is outstanding topped with Tropical Barbecue Sauce, then dipped in Bleu Cheese dressing.

Deadman's Fingers

Lambswool (bathing sponge)

Sponges come in various shapes, colors, and sizes. They are filter feeding animals, processing vast amounts of water through their systems daily.

Chicken 'n Beer

Chicken pieces—legs, wings, thighs, breasts, enough to feed your crew
Margarine—about 1/2 tablespoon per piece
Lawry's Seasoned Salt to taste
Pepper to taste
1 can beer, unless you're making a huge amount

1. Preheat oven to 350° F. Skin chicken, if desired.
2. In a single layer, place chicken on flat open pan. Place a piece of margarine on top of each piece of chicken, generously salt and pepper the poultry. Pour in enough beer so 1/2-3/4 inch stands in the pan. Drink the rest!
3. Bake chicken about 1 hour, or until done. Turn chicken pieces over twice during baking so they don't dry out.
4. Serve immediately. My dogs love the leftover liquid poured on their dry food.

Grilled Marinated Chicken

Serves 4-6

8   pieces chicken (skinned if desired)
3/4 cup cider vinegar
1   teaspoon salt
1   teaspoon pepper
1   tablespoon poultry seasoning
1   raw egg, well beaten
1/2 cup oil

1. Starting with vinegar, combine all ingredients, blend well.
2. Place chicken in a plastic bag, pour marinade over. Squeeze out excess air and seal. Marinate 4-24 hours, turning once or twice during process to redistribute liquid. Place bag in a bowl as a precaution against leaks. Refrigerate.
3. Cook on outdoor grill, over medium heat, about 40 minutes or until done. Baste with marinade during cooking. Serve at once.

Chicken Cacciatore a la Trigg Adams

Serves 6-8

2	chickens, cut up and dried off
1	cup olive oil
2	tablespoons celery, chopped
4	bay leaves
1 1/2	cups white wine
1	teaspoon salt
6	fillets of anchovies
2	cups chicken broth
1	medium onion, chopped
2	tablespoons parsley, chopped
2	cloves garlic, minced
1/2	teaspoon fresh ground rosemary
4	tablespoons wine vinegar
1	teaspoon pepper
3	tablespoons tomato paste

Sand Pine

Rice

1 1/2	cups rice
3	cups water
1	teaspoon salt
1/2	onion
1	teaspoon olive oil

1. Pour olive oil into earthen casserole or large, deep skillet. Very lightly brown chicken pieces and remove.
2. Sauté celery, onion, parsley, and then garlic in remaining oil.
3. Add most of chicken broth and allow to heat while you mix anchovies with tomato paste. Gradually thin tomato paste with remaining broth so that it won't lump as you add it to main sauté/broth.
4. Now add white wine, wine vinegar, rosemary, and bay leaves.
5. When good and hot, add chicken so that it is covered, and simmer for at least 45 minutes.
6. Clean up mess while boiling water for rice.
7. Add salt and a little butter or a teaspoon of olive oil to boiling water, and then add rice. Keep the heat up fairly high while stirring absolutely minimally, until surface of water is just below surface of rice.
8. Lower heat to absolute lowest simmer, push flat side of 1/2 onion down into rice, and cover very tightly, for 18 minutes. Be sure to save and freeze leftover broth, and add it to future batches.
9. Serve chicken over rice accompanied with bread to soak up broth.

Forty Thieves Chicken

Serves 4

4 chicken breasts (skinned optional)
2 tablespoons margarine
1/2 cup onion, chopped
2-3 teaspoons grated orange rind (2 oranges)
1 cup orange juice
1/4 cup honey
2 tablespoons curry powder
3 tablespoons sesame seeds
Salt and pepper (optional)

1. Preheat oven to 350° F.
2. In a small skillet, sauté onion in margarine until translucent. Put aside.
3. Grate peel from oranges while they are whole. Grate, halve, then juice oranges. Two Florida oranges give you about a cup of juice. Mix juice, peel, honey, sesame seeds, and sautéd onions together.
4. Lay chicken in a baking pan. Pour citrus mixture over.
5. Bake for 1 hour or until done, basting occasionally,

Mississippi Chicken

Serves 4-6

8 pieces chicken (skinned optional)
2 large green peppers, sliced
2 large onions, sliced (tennis ball size)
3 cloves garlic, crushed
4 Key limes or Persian limes
1/2 cup black olives
6 1/2 ounce jar marinated artichoke hearts
1/4 cup margarine
Soy sauce
Salt and pepper
1 loaf French bread

1. Preheat oven to 375° F.
2. In a large oven-proof roasting pan, or Dutch oven with lid, place a layer of onions and green peppers. Then lay on chicken pieces. Add peppers, onions, garlic, olives, and artichoke hearts, including juice. Slice margarine and scatter pats around. Sprinkle on soy sauce, salt and pepper. Squeeze on lime juice and lime pulp.
3. Cover. Bake 1 hour until chicken is tender.
4. Serve with French bread to soak up the broth.

Chicken Kiev

Serves 4

6   tablespoons butter
4   chicken breasts, boned
Parsley
Garlic powder
Salt and pepper
Flour
1   egg, beaten
Bread crumbs

1.   Cut butter into four 1 1/2 tablespoon sections. Form into four individual finger shapes to be rolled inside each chicken breast. Place in refrigerator to chill.

2.   Place each breast between 2 pieces of waxed paper. Pound thin. Remove top piece of waxed paper. Sprinkle each breast with parsley, garlic powder, salt and pepper. Lay one chilled, finger-shaped piece of butter onto a flattened breast. Fold sides inward and roll up like a package. Roll breast in flour. Repeat for the remaining breasts.

3.   Mix beaten egg with 1 tablespoon water. Dip each rolled breast into the egg mixture, then roll in bread crumbs. Place breasts in freezer for 30 minutes.

4.   Fry in deep fat (350° F) until golden about 7-10 minutes.

The Puncture Vine has bright yellow flowers and a spiny seed which can pierce a tennis shoe.

Tropical Chicken

Serves 4

4   chicken breasts (skinned optional)
3   oranges
2-3   yams
1/4   cup margarine, melted
1/4   cup rum
1/4   cup honey
1   teaspoon salt
1/2   teaspoon pepper
1/4   teaspoon ginger
1   cup coconut, shredded

Periwinkles

1.   Preheat oven to 350° F.
2.   Lay breasts in large flat oven-proof pan.
3.   Peel and section oranges over a bowl to catch juice. Squeeze juice left in the remnant of orange into the bowl containing the sections. Set aside.
4.   Slice yams and lay around chicken breasts.
5.   Melt margarine, add to orange sections. Stir in rum, honey, ginger, salt and pepper. Pour over chicken. Top with coconut.
6.   Bake about 1 hour or until chicken and yams are done.

Pineapple Chicken

Serves 4

4   chicken breasts (skinned optional)
2-3   tablespoons oil
1/3-1/2   cup brown sugar
1/2   cup vinegar
1/2   teaspoon salt
1/2   teaspoon ginger
1   teaspoon soy sauce
2   tablespoons cornstarch
8 1/4   ounce can chunk pineapple in syrup
1   fresh orange, sectioned
1   green pepper, cut in strips
1/3   cup maraschino cherries

1.   Heat oil in skillet. Brown chicken.
2.   Combine brown sugar, vinegar, salt, ginger, and soy sauce. Pour over chicken, cover and simmer 40 minutes.

3. Mix cornstarch with a small amount of pineapple syrup. Pour pineapple and syrup, orange, green pepper, and cherries into skillet. Stir in cornstarch mixture. Bring to a boil. Reduce heat. Cover. Simmer about 10 minutes longer or until chicken is tender.
4. Serve over rice. See Rice Basics recipe.

Boiled, Broiled, Spicy Hot Chicken With Marmalade

Serves 4

1 whole chicken
Salt and pepper
Tabasco sauce
Orange marmalade

1. Boil whole chicken in water for about 1 hour or until tender, but not falling apart. Remove from broth (save for Tail Waggin' Dog Soup), cut in half lengthwise. Lay skin side up on a broiling pan. Sprinkle with salt and pepper. Move oven racks down, away from heat source so skin can get brown and crisp, but not burned on the high places. In about 10-15 minutes skin will be golden and crispy.
2. Place on platter. Sprinkle on as much Tabasco as you can handle. Then spread marmalade on top. Serve immediately.

Wing 'N Wing
(Turkey Winglettes)

Serves 4

Wingettes or Winglettes are the meaty drumstick section of the wing.

4   turkey wingettes
4   tablespoons margarine
Salt and pepper to taste

Melt margarine in a skillet, add wingettes. Brown over medium heat. When golden add enough water so pan is 1/2 full. Season. Cover. Simmer about 2 1/2-3 hours or until meat falls from the bone. This can't be hurried because these wings are tough!

Cornish Hens Greek Style

Serves 2-4

2   Cornish hens split in half lengthwise (skinned optional)
1/4 cup melted margarine
Salt and pepper to taste
1   teaspoon oregano
1   clove garlic, crushed

1. Preheat oven to 350° F.
2. Place hens in baking dish. Rub with garlic clove, season with salt and pepper. Combine oregano with margarine. Pour over hens. Baste with margarine and oregano mixture every 15 minutes until done. Bake about 45 minutes to 1 hour.

Moist, Crispy Duck Without the Greasies

Serves 2-4

A personal friend who is a chef at a well-known restaurant shared this with me.

1   duck
1   onion
1   stalk celery
Parsley
1   small apple, quartered
Salt and pepper to taste

1. Rinse duck and pierce skin numerous times with a fork. Place in a large pot with a lid. Add enough water to cover 2/3 of the duck. Toss in remaining ingredients, cover, and bring to a boil—reduce heat to a medium boil. Turn bird occasionally while cooking to prevent sticking and promote even cooking. Test with a fork for doneness and tenderness. Cook about 1 1/2 hours.
2. When bird is done, remove from broth, cut in half lengthwise. Place skin side up on a broiler pan. Sprinkle with salt and pepper.
3. Move oven rack as far from the heat source as possible. You want a crispy golden skin—not burned places. Watch the bird closely, but it usually takes about 20 minutes. Time varies because of distance from the heat source. Skin will become golden and crispy while the meat remains moist and tender.
4. Serve with rice and Apple Walnut Sauté.

Marinated Grilled Pork Loin

Serves 2 hardy eaters or 4 good friends

1   pound pork tenderloin
Marinade:
1/4 cup fresh Key lime juice
1   clove garlic, crushed
1   teaspoon fresh peppergrass seeds* (optional)
1/4 teaspoon ground ginger
1/2 cup brown sugar, firmly packed
1/4 cup dark rum
1/8 cup soy sauce

1.   Blend above ingredients. Place pork in a plastic bag and pour in marinade. Twist tie closed. Place bag in bowl. Refrigerate. Turn occasionally to disperse marinade. Marinate 2 hours.
2.   Grill the pork on outside grill—a medium-low to low heat for about 30-40 minutes until done. Brush occasionally with the marinade. Save leftover marinade for sauce below. The internal temperature of pork should be 175° F to 180° F.

Sauce:
1/4 cup orange juice
1/2 cup water
1   tablespoon cornstarch
Remaining marinade

In a small sauce pan dissolve the cornstarch in a small amount of the water to prevent lumping. Add the remaining water, orange juice, and marinade. Thicken over medium heat stirring constantly. Pour the sauce over the pork loin just before serving. This sauce may also be served over noodles.

*Peppergrass is a common roadside weed native to the United States and Caribbean. It tastes similar to raw mustard greens. You may substitute pepper.

The Decorator Crab is a master of camouflage by attaching plants and shells to its hairy shell.

Pork Chops Au Rhum*

Serves 4-6

6   pork chops or pieces of chicken
Oil
3/4 cup boiling water
2/3 cup Sunmaid Brand Dried Fruit Bits or chopped dried apricots
1/2 cup maple syrup
1-2 tablespoons rum
1/4 teaspoon thyme
1   teaspoon salt
Pepper to taste

1.   Plump fruit in water 10 minutes.
2.   In a large skillet with lid, brown chops in a small amount of oil.
3.   Add syrup and rum to fruit/water mixture. Pour over chops. Add seasonings. Cover. Simmer 1 hour. Serve hot over rice. See Rice Basics recipe.

*Chicken may be substituted for chops.

Honey Lime Roast Pork

Serves 6

2 1/2-3 pounds pork tenderloin
2   tablespoons cognac
1/2   cup honey
2   cloves garlic, crushed
1/2   teaspoon ground ginger
1/4   teaspoon ground cloves
1   teaspoon salt
1/4   teaspoon pepper
Juice of Key lime

1.   Preheat oven to 350° F.
2.   Lightly score the surface of the roast with a sharp knife, making diagonal lines, ending with a diamond-shaped pattern.
3.   Combine the remaining ingredients in a small bowl. Spoon over the roast. Roast about 35 minutes per pound, basting occasionally. Serve immediately.

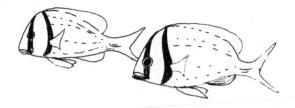

Pork Fish

Pork and Sauerkraut

Serves 6

2-3 pounds boneless pork loin, cut into 1-2 inch cubes
2 large onions, chopped
Oil
1 jar or package sauerkraut, 28-32 ounces
2-3 teaspoons tarragon
2 tablespoons caraway seeds
1 cup white wine
Salt and pepper
1 pint sour cream
Rye bread and butter

1. In a large pot with a lid, brown pork and onion in oil.
2. In a second pot add water and boil sauerkraut. Drain. Repeat. This eliminates the sour bite of the cabbage. Combine the drained sauerkraut and pork mixture. Add tarragon, caraway seeds, salt, pepper, and wine. Bring to a boil. Reduce heat. Simmer until pork is tender about 45 minutes to 1 hour. Add more wine if needed.
3. Serve with rye bread and butter. Sour cream is used to top each individual serving.

Spotted Eagle Ray

Piquant Beef au Jus

Serves 6

3   pound roast, California style or chuck, the thicker the better
Yellow mustard
1   lime
2   medium onions
2   tablespoons capers
2-3 tablespoons Worcestershire sauce
1   tablespoon light brown sugar
A few shakes Tabasco sauce
Margarine
4-5 large potatoes, quartered
4-5 large carrots, quartered
Salt and pepper to taste

1.   Preheat oven to 300° F. This roast may be cooked in a shallow baking dish with lid, a clay pot the top and bottom of which have been soaked 15 minutes in water prior to cooking, or a huge piece of heavy duty broiler foil, large enough to envelop the entire roast and contents with a generous seal.
2.   Lay roast in cooking vessel of your choice, spread thin layer of mustard on both sides, squeeze on lime juice.
3.   Thin slice onions, crush capers, spread on top of roast. Sprinkle on remaining ingredients. Dot with margarine. Surround with potatoes and carrots. Cover with lid or seal foil with double folds.
4.   Bake 3 hours. Serve hot. A complete meal.

Caution—if you use foil, open carefully, escaping steam can burn your hands.

Fruity Pot Roast

Serves 6

3-4	pounds chuck or rump roast
1 1/2	cups onions, sliced
12	dried apricots
1/4	cup raisins
12	dried apples
1	cup apple cider
2	tablespoons sugar
1/4	teaspoon cinnamon
1/8	teaspoon cloves
1/4	teaspoon ginger

1.   In a large Dutch oven, brown roast in its own trimmed fat. Add onions. Cook until limp. Add remaining ingredients. Cover. Simmer 2-2 1/2 hours or until meat is tender.

Marinated London Broil

London Broil or Flank steak—big enough to feed your crew
Worcestershire sauce, about 1/4 cup
1 garlic clove, crushed
Salt and pepper to taste

1.   Place steak in a shallow pan, large enough to hold the meat comfortably. Spread crushed garlic on both sides. Pour on Worcestershire sauce, enough so meat lies in some liquid, turn meat over so both sides are coated. Cover with plastic wrap. Refrigerate. Marinate at least one hour, turning once halfway through the process.
2.   Cook on barbecue grill the way you like it, baste with marinade.
3.   Cut in thin slices, serve immediately.

Charcoaled Eye Round

1	eye round roast—estimate about 1/3 pound per person
1/4	cup ground black pepper
1/2	cup table salt
1	clove garlic, crushed
1 1/2	tablespoons ground ginger

Charcoal fire with cover

1.   Roast should be room temperature. Pierce roast with holes 1/2 inch deep using a sharp knife.
2.   Mix pepper, salt, garlic, and ginger, and rub into roast. Let rest for 1 hour. Meat will look sandy with its salt coating.
3.   Prepare a charcoal fire in a covered grill. When coals glow (white hot), arrange a depression in them big enough to accommodate the roast. Lay the roast directly on the coals and close lid. Eye rounds have three sides, the roast should cook 10-12 minutes on each side, a total of 30-36 minutes. Long, thinner cuts cook 10 minutes. Shorter, broader cuts cook 12 minutes. When done, the center will be pink and juicy, getting progressively more done toward the outside surface.
4.   Remove from fire, brush off salt mixture, and slice. Serve at once.

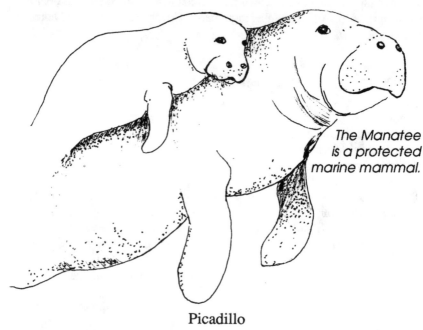

The Manatee
is a protected
marine mammal.

Picadillo

Serves 4

2   pounds ground chuck
2   medium onions, chopped
1   large green pepper, chopped
1   clove garlic, crushed
1   tablespoon horseradish
1   tablespoon mustard
1   large can tomatoes, partially drained
Salt and pepper to taste
2   tablespoons brown sugar
1/2 cup stuffed green olives
1/3 cup raisins
1/4 cup vinegar
1   tablespoon capers
3/4 cup red wine

In a large pot, sauté beef, add onions, peppers, and garlic. Cook until vegetables are limp. Add remaining ingredients. Cover. Simmer about 1 hour until mixture has a meat sauce like consistency. Serve over white rice with black beans and Cuban bread.

Charged-Up Meatloaf

Serves 4

1   pound ground sirloin
1/2   cup onions, chopped
1/2   cup green peppers, chopped
1   tablespoon horseradish
1   egg, beaten
1   teaspoon mustard
1/4   cup milk
1   cup bread crumbs
2/3   cup Buccaneer Barbecue Sauce (see recipe), or a commercial
      barbecue sauce

1.   Preheat oven to 400° F.
2.   Combine all ingredients with your hands except 1/3 cup of the barbecue sauce. In a baking pan, form into a loaf shape. Pour remaining sauce on top.
3.   Bake 1 hour. Serve immediately.

Cow Fish

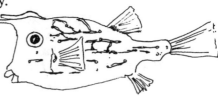

Untraditional Chili

Serves 6

2   tablespoons margarine
2   pounds ground chuck
2   large onions, chopped
2   large green peppers, chopped
1   garlic clove, crushed
2   cans whole tomatoes, each can 28 ounce size
2   cans red kidney beans, each can 19 ounce size
2   tablespoons sugar
Bird pepper (optional)
Salt and pepper to taste
Chili powder to taste

1.   Melt margarine in a Dutch oven-sized pot, add ground beef, onions, green pepper, and garlic. Sauté until done.
2.   Drain kidney beans and add to meat. Add tomatoes undrained, stir in. Add sugar, salt, pepper, and chili powder to taste. Bird pepper or chili pepper optional. Bring to a boil. Then turn to low heat. Cover.
3.   Simmer about one hour.

Stuffed Grape Leaves with Avgolemono Sauce

Serves 4

1/2 cup rice, uncooked
1   tablespoon margarine
1   pound ground chuck
1   medium large onion, finely chopped
1   garlic clove, crushed
1/2 teaspoon basil
1/2 teaspoon cinnamon
Salt and pepper to taste
1   jar grape leaves
1/4 cup lemon juice

1.   Wash rice until the water is clear to make it as starch free as possible. Place rice in a sauce pan with a tight-fitting lid, add margarine and 1 cup water. Bring to a boil uncovered, reduce heat to low, cover, cook until all water is absorbed—about 20 minutes.
2.   Mix all remaining ingredients except the grape leaves and lemon juice. Go easy on any salt in this recipe as the grape leaves are preserved in a salty brine. Add cooked rice to meat mixture.
3.   Open the jar of grape leaves and rinse. Pat dry. Lay leaf shiny side down, with the stem toward you. Put a small amount of filling on the leaf. Fold sides inward and roll up like a package. Lay stuffed grape leaves in a heavy sauce pan with lid. Pour on lemon juice, add about 1 cup water. Cover. Cook slowly about 45 minutes. Do not let them go dry. If needed, add more water.

Avgolemono Sauce

4   egg yolks
Juice of 1 lemon
1 1/4   cups liquid, cooked from stuffed grape leaves
1   tablespoon cornstarch

1.   Beat yolks well with a mixer. Carefully stir cornstarch into lemon juice (no lumps please). Then mix into egg yolks.
2.   Remove stuffed grape leaves to platter. Measure out about 1 1/4 cup liquid from pan. In a small sauce pan slowly combine yolk mixture and liquid. Cook over medium low heat until thickened. Pour over hot stuffed grape leaves. Serve immediately.

Wild Petunias have lavender-blue flowers.

Hawaiian Pepper Steak

Serves 4

1 1/2	pounds sirloin steak 1 inch thick, sliced thin
Oil	
3	large green peppers, sliced
1	cup onion, sliced
1	clove garlic, crushed
1/2	teaspoon pepper
1	teaspoon ginger
1/2	teaspoon brown sugar
3	tablespoons soy sauce
3/4	cup beef bouillon
1	tablespoon cornstarch
1	small can unsweetened chunk pineapple in its own juice, drained (8 ounce)
2	cups rice, cooked

1. In a large skillet sauté garlic, ginger, and pepper in oil. Remove and discard garlic when it turns golden. Stir fry steak and onions, add ginger, brown sugar, soy sauce, beef bouillon. Simmer. Dissolve cornstarch in 1 tablespoon water, slowly stir in to thicken. Add green pepper and pineapple. Simmer about 3 minutes or until pepper is cooked to your taste.
2. Serve over rice.

*Beef Teriyaki Kabobs

Serves 4

2 1/2-3 pounds sirloin, marinated
1 carton cherry tomatoes
1 large can pineapple chunks unsweetened in its own juice
(20 ounces)
1 or 2 large green peppers
Onions, quartered
Skewers**

Marinade:
1/2 teaspoon ginger
1/4 cup sherry
1/2 teaspoon pepper
1/2 cup soy sauce
1/2 cup pineapple juice (from can)
2 tablespoons brown sugar
2 tablespoons onion, grated
1 clove garlic, crushed

1. To make marinade, combine all ingredients. Cut steak into cubes. Place in a plastic bag. Pour on marinade. Twist tie closed. Place in bowl in refrigerator. Marinate 2-4 hours. Turn occasionally to disperse marinade.
2. Alternate veggies, fruit, and meat on skewers. Cook over gas or charcoal grill until done to your taste.

*May substitute chicken
**Many times these are free from your butcher or grocery store meat department.

Cajun Stuffed Peppers

Serves 4

2   large green peppers
1/2 pound ground chuck
1/4 cup rice, cooked
1/2 cup onion, finely chopped
1/2 teaspoon Jane's Krazy Mixed Up Salt
3   tablespoons catsup
Pepper to taste
1   can (14 1/2 ounce) Cajun-style stewed tomatoes
1   tablespoon brown sugar
1/2 cup raisins

1. Preheat oven to 350° F.
2. Cut peppers in half lengthwise, clean out insides.
3. Combine beef, rice, onion, salt, and catsup. Fill peppers with mixture. Season meat mixture with ground pepper.
4. In a shallow oven-proof pan, mix Cajun tomatoes, brown sugar, and raisins. Place peppers in sauce. Cover with aluminum foil.
5. Bake 30 minutes covered. Remove foil and bake an additional 10 minutes to brown meat. Serve immediately.

Bomancoo Beef Stew

Serves 4

2 pounds beef chuck, cut in pieces
1/4 cup flour
1/2 teaspoon garlic salt
1/2 teaspoon celery salt
1 teaspoon salt
1/2 teaspoon ginger
1/2 teaspoon cinnamon
1/4 teaspoon pepper
Oil
15 ounce can whole tomatoes
1/2 cup celery, chopped
1 cup onions, chopped
3 tablespoons cider vinegar
2 tablespoons molasses
1 cup carrot, cut up
1/4 cup raisins
1 cup sweet potato, cut up

Combine flour, garlic salt, celery salt, salt, ginger, cinnamon, and pepper. Coat beef. In a large pot or Dutch oven, brown beef in hot oil. Stir in remaining ingredients. Bring to a boil then reduce heat. Cover and simmer about 1 1/2-2 hours or until beef is tender.

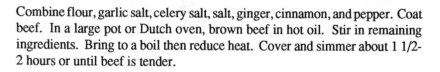

Country Pot Pie

Serves 6

1 pound ground chuck
1/3 cup milk
1 egg
1/2 teaspoon basil
1 cup bread crumbs
1/2 clove garlic, crushed
1 pound potatoes
1/2 pound onions
Oil
2 teaspoons parsley
1 large tomato, sliced
1/2 cup cheddar cheese, grated
Salt and pepper to taste

1. Preheat oven to 325° F.
2. In a large mixing bowl, combine ground chuck, milk, egg, basil, bread crumbs, garlic, 1 teaspoon salt, and pepper to taste. Blend well. Press gently into a 9 inch pie plate. Form a rim around the edge.
3. Slice potatoes 1/4 inch thick, peeling is optional. Steam or cook in a small amount of water until done but firm. Drain. Stir in 1/2 teaspoon salt and all parsley. Pepper to taste.
4. Slice onions. Sauté in small amount of oil until soft and transparent.
5. Alternate layers of potatoes, onions, and tomato, in pie plate. Cover with aluminum foil, bake 25 minutes. Remove foil, top with cheese. Return to oven 5-10 minutes or until cheese melts. Serve at once.

Caribbean Curried Goat

Serves 6

Goat is a staple in the West Indies. It tastes like beef, but is tough so must be cooked a long time to tenderize. Goat may be substituted with chicken or beef, cooking 1 hour.

3	pounds goat, chicken, or beef—cut into bite-size pieces
3	tablespoons oil
3	tablespoons margarine
2 1/2	cups onion, chopped
4	tablespoons curry powder
1	tablespoon hot chili peppers, chopped
1/2	teaspoon allspice
1	cup blenderized fresh coconut or commercially prepared shredded coconut
1	cup water
2	chicken bouillon cubes
1	cup milk
1	bay leaf, crushed
2	tablespoons fresh lime juice

Salt and pepper to taste

1. In a 4 quart pot with lid, brown goat in oil. Add margarine and onions. Cook onions until soft. Stir in remaining ingredients. Cover. Simmer about 3 hours over low heat or until goat is tender. Add water if necessary. Serve hot over rice with some or all of the following "boys" sprinkled on top. See Rice Basics recipe.

Boys—these accompaniments were called boys because they were tradition-ally served in individual dishes by boys.

Mango chutney, peanuts, sliced bananas, pineapple chunks, shredded coconut, raisins, chopped hard-boiled eggs.

Southeastern Five-lined Skink

Sky Fried Squirrel

Serves 2

This game almost falls into the "road kill," department. Squirrels have a pesky habit of chewing on power lines. I have been told that once they start to get a tingle, it feels so good they just can't quit. Occasionally early in the morning I will hear the powerful hum and zap we all associate with electricity. I know another squirrel has "bitten it," so to speak. Depending on the intensity of the blast, they can be anywhere from slightly singed to partially cooked. These unfortunates are always lying directly under power lines. I'm not suggesting you eat road kills or other wildlife fatalities, but if you know a hunter, this is a real recipe. Marie Crawford, who regularly cooks game, swears it will make the oldest and orneriest squirrel as tender as a mother's smile.

2   squirrels, dressed and properly prepared
2   tablespoons margarine
1   cup Pepperidge Farm Herb Seasoned Stuffing
1/4   cup and 1 tablespoon water
1/2   cup onion chopped
1/4   cup celery, chopped
1/4   cup walnuts
1/2   teaspoon parsley
Poultry seasoning
2-4   strips bacon—depends on size of squirrel
Aluminum foil

1.   Preheat oven to 400° F.
2.   Put margarine and water in a medium sauce pan. Boil to melt margarine. Remove from heat. Stir in stuffing mix, onion, celery, walnuts, and parsley.
3.   Lay squirrels on their backs and place stuffing in cavities. Sprinkle with poultry seasoning. Lay 1 to 2 strips of bacon on top depending on squirrel size. Wrap tight in aluminum foil. Place in oven-proof dish.
4.   Bake for 1-1 1/4 hours depending on size of squirrel.

Sauteéd Lily Pad Loungers
(Frog legs)

Serves 4

2 pounds frog legs
Salt and pepper
Garlic powder
Lime juice
Cracker meal or bread crumbs
Margarine and oil

1. Sprinkle lime juice, salt, pepper, and garlic powder over frog legs. Roll in cracker meal.
2. Sauté in margarine and oil combination until done (margarine for flavor; oil doesn't burn as easily). Turn oven on lowest setting with door open. Lay out frog legs on a cookie sheet. Store in oven until ready to serve.

Free Range Frogs Tempura

Serves 4

2 pounds frog legs
8 ounce box Jiffy Buttermilk Biscuit Mix
10 ounce bottle soda water
Salt and pepper
Garlic powder
Oil

1. Salt and pepper legs, sprinkle on garlic powder.
2. Pour about 2-2 1/2 inches oil in a deep pot. Heat on medium high setting.
3. Sift dry Jiffy Mix into bowl. Add about 1/2 cup soda water. Stir in, trying to stir out lumps. The consistency should be like cake batter. You'll probably need a bit more soda water. Go slowly.
4. When batter is correct, drop a tiny amount into hot oil. It should puff up and rise immediately to the surface. If it doesn't, the oil is not hot enough. When oil is ready, dip frog legs into batter, then lower into oil. When they are golden, remove onto a cookie sheet lined with paper towels.
5. Place cookie sheet in the oven, which is set on the lowest setting to keep warm. Leave door open so legs will stay crispy. Serve with Tiger Sauce.

Eastern Diamond-back Rattlesnake

Cabbage Palm Chicken
(Rattlesnake)

Serves lots because most people
are too nervous to eat much.

It is important to check the snake to make sure it hasn't bitten itself in the struggle. This contaminates the meat.

1 rattlesnake
Key lime or sour orange juice
Salt and pepper
Whisper of ginger
Oil
Cornmeal
Flour

1.   Clean snake by carefully removing head and skin. Remove entrails and wash thoroughly. Cut in 1 inch sections.
2.   Marinate meat in juice, pepper, and ginger for 3-4 hours.
3.   Remove from marinade, pat dry. Mix equal amounts of cornmeal and flour. Coat snake, sprinkle on salt and pepper. Fry in oil about 5 minutes until golden. Do not overcook. Snake can get tough.

Drying the Skin

Stretch and tack the skin inside toward you. Cover with a layer of baking soda. Store at room temperature for about 10 days. Use glycerine to soften the skin.

Stuffed Breadfruit

Serves 4

Prepare Roasted Breadfruit recipe.

1.   Cut off top jack-o-lantern like. Remove pithy core and discard. Allow to cool awhile. Scoop out inside.
2.   Mix cooked breadfruit with about 1-2 cups warm Picadillo (see recipe). Stuff it all back into the shell. Return to oven (or charcoals for outdoor cooking) for 15 minutes.

Greens
and Other Perishables

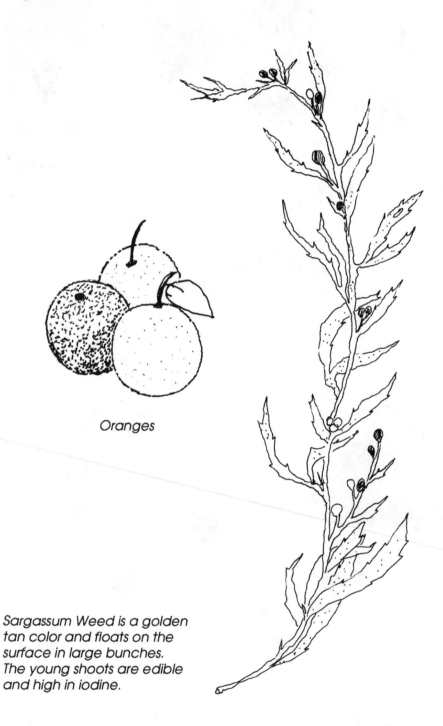

Oranges

Sargassum Weed is a golden
tan color and floats on the
surface in large bunches.
The young shoots are edible
and high in iodine.

Oranges—Florida Gold

Ponce de Leon probably introduced the orange to Florida in 1513 while searching for the Fountain of Youth. He and his crew were unaware that they were shaping our destiny by indiscriminately scattering seeds throughout the fertile land. Much later, realizing the orange's importance, Spain passed a law requiring each Spanish sailor to carry 100 orange seeds to the new world.

This fruit was so revered during the fifteenth century that Charles VII of France built the first orangerie, an elaborate hothouse devoted totally to propagating oranges. Most orangerie were elaborately vaulted galleries with great glass windows facing south. Potted trees sat on floors honeycombed with openings. Below, huge pans of water simmered over open fires, and steam rose through the floor vents creating a tropical atmosphere for the trees above.

Florida's real development began in the early 1800s when Andrew Jackson illegally entered Florida, a Spanish territory, under the guise of hunting Indians and returning runaway slaves to their owners. Spain simply could not protect a land so distant, and by 1821 Florida had been wrested from Spanish control. Jackson, our first Governor, opened the territory to American settlers, and so began the Florida Gold Rush. But our gold grew on trees—orange trees.

With the Armed Occupation Act in 1842 and subsequently the Homestead Act granting 160 acres of free land to hardy souls who would farm, improve, and continuously occupy the land, Florida was settled. Growing oranges was a natural.

Then came Flagler's Florida East Coast Railroad. No longer were growers at the fickle mercy of wind, weather, and boats. Flagler even devised a way to warn growers of a hard frost. His train engineers steaming through the bucolic landscape would give a long continuous whistle—an ominous forewarning. Even this didn't save North Florida grove owners from two brutal back-to-back freezes in the winter of 1894-95. They were wiped out. Many left the state disillusioned, but some pioneering souls moved south, ever downward on the peninsula, eventually settling the famous Indian River country, to begin again.

Today Florida grows about one-fourth of the world's oranges aided by advanced technology which allows trees to produce marketable fruit within three to five years.

Citrus is a fruit which is truly tree-ripened. Once it's picked, ripening stops and aging begins. This is why all citrus belongs in the refrigerator, not a decorative fruit bowl. Improper storage only promotes decay and loss of vitamin C.

Oranges are tropical tricksters. The color of an orange does not indicate ripeness. Even though they are ready to be harvested, oranges may still be green, basking in the sun like a tourist. Exposure to cold stimulates production of ethylene, turning the fruits orange. Early in the season when we have not yet experienced cool evenings, harvested oranges are placed in "de-greening" rooms and subjected to low levels of ethylene to induce color change.

Just after World War II a discovery was made which revolutionized citrus consumption—frozen concentrate. It is fresh juice, boiled to a high viscosity in a vacuum, separated into several components, reassembled, then frozen solid. It's not only convenient, but consistent in color and flavor. Natural juice can be unpredictable, so if you don't like surprises, use concentrate.

Substituting pure undiluted concentrate for the same amount of juice in baking gives a stronger orange flavor. I drink fresh-squeezed juice, but I cook with concentrate.

Nothing in citrus is wasted. In addition to food products, citrus is also used in perfume, cosmetics, pharmaceuticals, paints, insecticides, textiles, and more. Cooking oil can be refined from the seeds, and the pulp is used as cattle feed.

When Ponce de Leon returned to Florida in 1521, he landed on the West coast, probably around Charlotte Harbor. He received an unfriendly reception by the Indians, was hit by an arrow, and later died. He was buried in Puerto Rico.

He came to take—in search of gold, slaves, and the Fountain of Youth. Instead he gave—oranges, our number-one cash crop, and our name, Florida. Ultimately he gave his life and shaped our future forever.

Types of Florida Oranges

Hamlin—An early-season orange, usually has few seeds, an excellent juice orange. (October-December)

Pineapple—Midseason orange, smooth skin, has some seeds. Sweet and juicy. (December-February)

Valencia—A late-season orange. Thin skin, oval shape, and deep orange color. Usually no more than six seeds. (February-June)

Tangerine—Small or medium size, flat at ends. Deep orange or red color with few seeds. Zipper skin fruit, peels and sections easily. (November-January)

Honey Orange—Unusually sweet and juicy. It is a member of the orange family, though it looks like a large tangerine and peels easily. (February-April)

Temple—Medium to large size, deep orange color, oval shape. Sometimes has pebbly skin, peels and sections easily. (December-March)

Orange Blossom Carrots

Serves 6

2 1/2-3   cups sliced carrot rounds
1/4   cup sugar
1/4   teaspoon salt
Whisper each ground cloves and ginger

1 1/2   tablespoons cornstarch
1   cup orange juice
1   tablespoon margarine

1. Steam or cook carrots until tender. Drain. Pour into serving bowl. Cover.
2. In a sauce pan, combine all dry ingredients, blend well. Add orange juice and margarine. Cook over medium heat, stirring constantly until thick.
3. Pour over carrots. Serve at once.

Honey Glazed Carrots

Serves 4

16 tiny whole carrots—about 4 inches long
1/4 cup margarine
Salt to taste
1/2 cup honey
Whisper of ginger

1. Boil carrots until tender. Drain.
2. In a large skillet melt margarine. Stir in remaining ingredients, then cooked carrots. Simmer slowly until carrots are glazed and golden brown. Serve at once.

Curry Baked Tomatoes

Serves 4

2   large ripe tomatoes
Oil
1/2 teaspoon curry powder—can use more
Salt to taste
1/2 cup sharp cheddar cheese, grated
1/2 cup Pepperidge Farm Herb Seasoned Stuffing
1/4 cup melted margarine
3/4 teaspoon basil
1/8 teaspoon pepper

1. Preheat oven to 350° F.
2. Wash and halve tomatoes. Brush skin with oil. Place cut side up in a baking dish. Sprinkle sliced side of each tomato with salt and 1/8 teaspoon curry.
3. In a small bowl combine cheese, dry stuffing, melted margarine, basil, and pepper. Cover the tops of the tomatoes with this mixture.
4. Bake 15-20 minutes. Serve at once.

Cherry Tomato Sauté

Serves 4

1	container (little green basket) fresh cherry tomatoes
2-4	tablespoons butter
1/2-1	teaspoon basil

Salt and pepper

1. Wash tomatoes and dry.
2. Melt butter in frying pan on medium heat. Add tomatoes. Sprinkle on basil, salt and pepper. Sauté about 5 minutes. Do not overcook. Serve at once.

Broccoli Beau Monde

Serves 4-6

1	large bunch fresh broccoli
3	tablespoons margarine
1/2	teaspoon Beau Monde seasoning
2	tablespoons dry white wine

1. Steam or cook broccoli in a small amount of salted water until tender.
2. Remove from pan, melt margarine, add wine and seasoning. Put broccoli back in pan and stir around to coat evenly. Serve at once.

NOTE: You may want to add more of the ingredients in the butter sauce, depending upon your taste.

Broccoli With Mayo

I know it sounds strange, but it is really very good. Same instructions as Broccoli Beau Monde for broccoli preparation. Instead of butter sauce, top with mayonnaise.

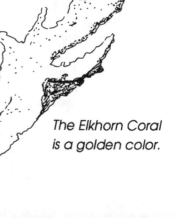

*The Elkhorn Coral
is a golden color.*

Tipsy Broccoli

Serves 4

1 large bunch fresh broccoli (about 1 pound)
Margarine
1-2 tablespoons white wine
Salt and pepper to taste

1. Prepare broccoli by trimming off long stalks and cutting into serving size pieces.
2. Steam until tender, about 10 minutes. Drain. Pour into serving bowl. Cover.
3. In the sauce pan, melt 2 or 3 tablespoons margarine (enough to coat broccoli to your liking) add wine, stir. Taste. Adjust seasonings. Pour over broccoli. Serve at once.

Broccoli Key Lime

Same as above but substitute 1-3 teaspoons, fresh squeezed lime juice for wine.

Salt-Water Corn on the Cob

Years ago in a ramshackle building on Key Largo, there was a restaurant called "Mac and Marie's." Old timers will remember it with deep affection. This is a take-off on one of Mac's recipes.

Ears of corn— enough to feed your crew
Salt water (seawater)*
Sugar
Salt and pepper
Butter or margarine

1. Pull back husks. Remove silk, recover with husks.
2. Pour salt water into a large vessel. Sprinkle in some sugar, about 2 tablespoons per gallon. Add corn. Refrigerate over night.
3. Corn may be boiled, steamed, microwaved, or roasted on a charcoal grill. Roasted is best, it gives the corn a faint smoky flavor. Place corn on rack, grill 3-5 minutes on each side, turning the corn so it roasts on four sides.
4. Serve hot, season with salt, pepper, and butter to taste.
*If ocean water is unavailable, health food stores carry sea salt, which is harvested by evaporating sea water.
1 tablespoon sea salt and 1 pint tap water=1 pint seawater
2 tablespoons sea salt and 1 quart tap water=1 quart seawater
1/4 cup sea salt and 1/2 gallon tap water=1/2 gallon seawater
1/2 cup sea salt and 1 gallon tap water=1 gallon seawater

The North American Crocodile is a shy reptile that lives in mangrove creeks.

Stuffed Christophene Squash

Serves 4-6

The Spanish call this squash Chayote, Caribbean Islanders, Christophene. You may substitute summer squash or zucchini.

3   medium Christophene, summer squash or zucchini, halved lengthwise, centers scooped out, seeds removed
1/2 cup onions, minced
1   cup celery, finely chopped
3-4 tablespoons margarine
1   ripe tomato, chopped (about 2-2 1/2 inches in diameter)
1   cup herb seasoned bread crumbs or Pepperidge Farm Herb Seasoned Stuffing
Salt and pepper to taste
1   cup cheddar cheese, shredded

1.   Simmer squash halves in water 5 minutes, drain. Preheat oven to 350° F.
2.   Sauté onions, celery, and margarine in sauce pan until celery is soft. Add tomato, bread crumbs, and seasonings, stirring well. Stir in cheese until melted. Fill squash.
3.   Lay squash in a shallow baking pan, add about 1/4 inch water. Bake 30 minutes. Serve immediately.

Acorn Squash With Raspberries

1/2 acorn squash per person
The following ingredients will go into *each* 1/2 squash in the second stage of baking.
1   tablespoon butter
2   tablespoons brown sugar
2   tablespoons Triple Sec
15   or so fresh or frozen raspberries

1.   Preheat oven to 350° F. Total baking time 1 hour.
2.   Wash squash. Cut in half. Remove seeds.
3.   Lay cut side down in a shallow baking pan. Add 1/2 inch water. Bake 45 minutes.
4.   Remove squash from oven. Flip squash over. Fill each empty seed cavity with the above ingredients using those amounts listed for each squash.
5.   Return to oven for 15 minutes. Serve immediately.

Jumby Bay Acorn Squash
(A Variation)

Substitute 2 tablespoons Jumby Bay Rum or any good rum for the Triple Sec and 3 grapefruit sections for the raspberries. Prepare as directed above.

Saucy Peas
(Peas In Onion Sauce)

Serves 4

1   box frozen peas (serves 4)
1   tablespoon margarine
1/2   cup onions, chopped
1   tablespoon flour
2/3   cup milk
1/4   teaspoon salt
Pepper to taste

1.   Prepare peas as directed on package. Meanwhile, prepare sauce.
2.   In a small sauce pan sauté onion in margarine until translucent and limp. Stir in flour, then slowly add milk, stirring constantly cooking until thick. Add salt and pepper to taste.
3.   Drain peas. Pour on sauce. Serve immediately.

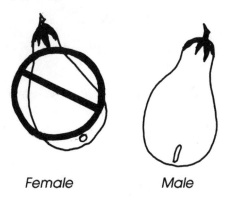

Female   Male

Fast Eddie's Macho Male Eggplant Stir Fry

Serves 6

Eddie Gurney (who keeps me presentable) owns Halo Haircutters in Coconut Grove. Going there is like stepping back in time. He works there with his son Eddie, wife Beverly, and daughter Beverly. In this recipe Eddie teaches us something about the birds and the bees. He says that "male" eggplants have an elongated bloom scar at the bottom, fewer seeds and are never bitter. So be sure to pick out a big "male," for this recipe—deep purple and very firm.

2   tablespoons olive oil
3   cloves garlic, minced
1/2 cup Spanish onion, slivered
5   cups (2) male eggplants, peeled and cut into 1 inch cubes
1/2 cup red bell pepper, cut into 1 inch pieces
1/2 cup yellow bell pepper, cut into 1 inch pieces
1/4 cup Cubanell peppers, cut up

Sauce
1/4 cup wine (any drinking wine will do)
2   tablespoons soy sauce
2   tablespoons balsamic vinegar
2   tablespoons brown sugar
3   healthy dashes Tabasco sauce
1   teaspoon sesame oil

1. Sauté onion and garlic in olive oil until transparent.
2. Add eggplant. While it is cooking (about 2-3 minutes), combine all ingredients to make sauce.
3. Add peppers and sauce. Stir fry until eggplant is done. Serve at once.

Sweet and Sour Green Beans

Serves 4

3 cups fresh green beans cut into 2 inch lengths
1/2 teaspoon salt
2 strips bacon
3 tablespoons onions, chopped
2 tablespoons sugar
2 tablespoons vinegar
1 teaspoon cornstarch
Salt and pepper

1. Place beans, 1/2 teaspoon salt and 1/3 cup water in a pot. Steam or cook covered for 15-20 minutes until done. Reserve 1/3 cup liquid from beans.
2. Meanwhile, fry bacon. Lay crisp bacon on a paper towel to drain. Using 1 tablespoon bacon grease, sauté onions until limp. Pour in 1/3 cup bean liquid, sugar, and vinegar. Stir over low heat. Dissolve cornstarch in a small amount of water. Stir in until sauce is thickened.
3. Pour over beans. Crumble bacon on top. Serve at once.

Golden Beets

Serves 4

2 cups cooked or canned beets, sliced
1/2 cup orange juice
1 tablespoon butter
Grated peel from 1 orange

1. Combine all ingredients, simmer but don't boil. Serve hot.

CAUTION—Do not grate orange down to the white skin. It's bitter.

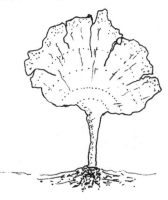

*Udotea Flabellum
is an olive green
marine algae.*

Sour Cream Mushrooms

Serves 4

1   pound fresh mushrooms—small are best
1   cup onion, chopped
1/4 cup margarine
1   teaspoon salt
1/4 teaspoon pepper
1/8 teaspoon nutmeg
1   tablespoon flour
1/2 teaspoon Worcestershire sauce
1   cup sour cream

1.   Wash and dry mushrooms. If they are large, slice them. Small ones can be left whole. Sauté with onion in margarine until onion is soft. Add salt, pepper, nutmeg, and flour stirring constantly. Cover, cook 5 minutes. Blend in Worcestershire sauce and sour cream. Heat, but do not boil. Serve at once.

Whipped Potatoes Supreme

Serves 6

1/2   cup onion, chopped
3-4   tablespoons margarine
2   cups water
2/3-1 cup sour cream
2   cups instant potato flakes
Salt and pepper to taste

Houses of Refuge were built along Florida's east coast in the 1870s to rescue shipwrecked mariners.

1. Preheat oven to 300° F.
2. In a 2-quart sauce pan, sauté onion in margarine until soft and transparent. Add water and heat to just below boiling. Stir in 2/3 cup sour cream. Pour in potato flakes, blend well. If it is too stiff, add more sour cream. Salt and pepper to taste.
3. Pour into a 1-quart casserole and bake for 20-30 minutes or until heated through. Serve hot. No one will ever guess these are instant.

Stuffed Baked Potatoes

Serves 4

4	baking potatoes
2	tablespoons butter
1/2	cup onion, chopped

Salt and pepper to taste
1/4-1/3 cup milk
Paprika
Grated cheddar cheese or butter (optional)

1. Preheat oven to 400° F. Scrub and bake potatoes 45-60 minutes or until fork tender. A microwave oven can be substituted. Potatoes should be cooked for 25-30 minutes (or 6-8 minutes per potato) with this method.
2. Melt 2 tablespoons butter in a skillet. Sauté onions until limp.
3. Halve potatoes lengthwise. Carefully scoop out potato so as not to damage skin. Mash potatoes with an electric mixer, add onions, salt and pepper to taste, and milk to the right consistency.
4. Fill potato shells. Top with a pat of butter and sprinkle with paprika, or top with grated cheese. Return to oven to melt cheese or bake tops golden about 5-10 minutes. Serve at once.

Count Dracula's Nightmare
(Garlic Potatoes)

Serves 4

As a rule of thumb, I figure about 1 potato per person and a clove of garlic per potato.

4   large potatoes, sliced with skins on (1/4 inch thick)
3-4 tablespoons margarine
4   cloves garlic, crushed
Salt and pepper to taste

1.   Steam or boil sliced potatoes until almost done. Shake potatoes off to remove excess water, and lay on paper towels.
2.   In a large skillet, melt margarine, add garlic. Over medium heat, lay potatoes in skillet. Turn frequently so they will not burn but will form a crisp, brown crust. Serve immediately.

Rice Basics

Serves 4-6

This recipe is easily reduced or increased. Always use twice as much water as rice—salt to taste.

1 1/2   cups uncooked rice (not minute rice)
3   cups water
1   teaspoon salt

1.   Rinse rice with water until water is quite clear. Drain.
2.   In a large sauce pan with a tight-fitting lid, add all above ingredients. Stir.
3.   Place uncovered on high heat. Bring to a boil. Stir. Reduce heat to low. Cover. Cook about 20 minutes or until all water is absorbed. Makes perfect rice every time.

Barred Owl

Simple Fried Rice

Serves 6

Make plain rice. See Rice Basics recipe, but omit salt.

6   strips bacon
3/4 cup onions, chopped
Soy sauce

1. Cut raw bacon into tiny pieces. Sauté bacon and onion together until bacon is crispy and onion golden.
2. Over medium to medium-low heat, add rice to bacon mixture, stir vigorously. Add soy sauce to taste. Enough soy sauce should be added to give rice the typical light brown color of fried rice. Serve at once.

Coconut Rice

Serves 4

3/4   cup rice, uncooked
1 1/2 cups water
1   teaspoon salt
1   tablespoon margarine
1/2   cup coconut, shredded

In a saucepan with a lid, combine all ingredients except coconut. Bring to a boil. Cover. Reduce heat to low. Simmer until all water is absorbed, about 20 minutes. Stir in coconut. Serve hot as a side dish.

Black Beans

Serves 6-8

If you are a purist, you can soak dried beans a day ahead, but I prefer instant gratification.

1   cup green pepper, chopped
1   cup onion, chopped
1   clove garlic, crushed
2   cans black beans, undrained
2   bay leaves, crumbled
Olive oil

1. Sauté green pepper, onion, and garlic in olive oil until soft. Add beans and bay leaves. Simmer 20-30 minutes.
2. Serve immediately with rice and chopped onions.

Small Dog Small Rope* Quiche

Serves 4 as a side dish

Eastern Caribbean vernacular for "live within your means." My cousin Darlene created this out of existing items she had at home one cold rainy evening when going to the store wasn't even a consideration. Hence the name.

9   inch pie shell *unbaked* (store-bought or see Memorable Pie Crust recipe)
Dijon mustard
1   onion, sliced
1/2 pound Raclette Cheese or Gruyere as a substitute, sliced
1   yellow tomato, sliced
Minced garlic
Oregano
Olive oil—hot pepper olive oil is best

1. Preheat oven to 350° F.
2. Spread a thin layer of Dijon mustard on pie crust. Bake for 10 minutes.
3. Sauté onion in hot pepper olive oil until onion is translucent.
4. Layer onto crust: onion, cheese, and tomato. Sprinkle on garlic and oregano. Drizzle on hot pepper olive oil, 1-2 teaspoons.
5. Bake for 30 minutes.

Apple Walnut Sauté

Serves 6

One apple per person
6   apples each cut into eighths
1/3 cup broken walnuts
4-6 tablespoons margarine
Whisper of salt
Cinnamon to taste
3-4 tablespoons honey

1. In a large skillet, melt margarine and sauté apples and walnuts about 10 minutes, stirring constantly to insure even cooking of apples. Undercooking them slightly lets the apples hold their shape and gives a firmer texture. Do not overcook.
2. Sprinkle on cinnamon, salt, and honey. Stir gently, taste. Adjust last three ingredients.
3. Serve immediately. Especially good with duck.

Green Banana Sauté

Serves 6

4   green bananas
1   medium onion (about 2 1/2 inches in diameter)
Salt and pepper to taste
Oil

1. To peel a green banana, slice ends off, cut banana in half crosswise. Make four lengthwise slits through the skin in each half, then pull peels off sideways. Cut banana into 1/4 inch thick round slices.
2. Thinly slice onion.
3. In a skillet, sauté onions and bananas over medium to medium-high heat, about 10 minutes. Onions will be clear and slightly golden. Season and serve hot. Tastes a lot like sautéed summer squash.

Baked Bananas

1 ripe banana per person

1. Preheat oven to 400° F.
2. Pierce bananas in a couple of places with the long tines of a meat fork. Do not peel.
3. Bake for 10-15 minutes, bananas will feel tender when squeezed. Serve hot as a vegetable or dessert.

Charcoaled Bananas

1 ripe banana per person

1. Wrap unpeeled banana in aluminum foil and lay on coals. Bake about 10-20 minutes. A time is tough on this one because temperatures vary.
2. Serve hot as vegetable or dessert.

Outward Bound Papaya Greens

Papaya greens can be somewhat bitter. This is definitely survival food. If you are ever marooned in a papaya grove, this knowledge might be invaluable; otherwise it is fun to know that papaya greens are edible.

Young papaya leaves
Salt and pepper
Butter
Sour cream
1 teaspoon horseradish

1.   Gather enough young papaya leaves for a "mess." This is a southern unit of measure—it's enough to feed your crew. Wash, trim off stems.
2.   Boil in salted water for 5 minutes. Drain. Repeat. This reduces the bitterness. Leaves should be cooked until tender. Season to taste.

Green Papaya Casserole

Serves 4

1	grapefruit sized green papaya
2	medium onions, sliced
2	tablespoons margarine
Salt to taste	
14 1/2	ounce can Cajun-style stewed tomatoes, undrained
1	tablespoon brown sugar
1	cup sour cream
1	Jalapeño pepper sliced
1 1/2	cups cheddar cheese, shredded

1.   Preheat oven to 350° F.
2.   Peel papaya and remove seeds. Slice thin. Put papaya in a covered sauce pan. Bring to a boil. Cook until fork tender, about 12-15 minutes. Drain.
3.   Sauté onions in margarine until soft.
4.   Combine cooked papaya, onions, tomatoes, brown sugar, salt, sour cream, Jalapeño, and all but 1/2 cup cheese. Pour into greased casserole dish. Top with remaining cheese.
5.   Bake 30 minutes or until bubbly.

Bubbly Broiled Grapefruit

Serves 4

2   large grapefruit, halved and seeds removed
1 1/2   teaspoon honey (per half)
1/2   teaspoon margarine (per half)
Whisper of cinnamon (per half)

Top each half with honey, margarine, and cinnamon. Place grapefruit halves in a shallow pan about 6-8 inches from the heat source and broil till bubbly. Serve as a side dish for dinner or for breakfast.

Roasted Breadfruit

Serves 4

"Why should I work in the bright hot sun when the breadfruit's free and the conch don't run?"—An eastern Caribbean saying.

West Indians roast their breadfruit outdoors on a coalpot, a hibachi-like device. Ripe breadfruit, roasted directly on the coals, is turned frequently to insure even cooking. It takes about 45 minutes. Genuine coalpots are difficult to locate, but ripe breadfruit can be roasted in the oven or outside on a charcoal grill. Outdoor cooking directly on the coals requires scraping off the burned outer skin of the breadfruit.

1 breadfruit

1.   Wrap it in two layers of aluminum foil. Bake at 375° F for 45 minutes.
2.   Cut in half. Remove pithy core. Scoop out vegetable. Season with salt, pepper, and butter.

Cattail Hearts

Cattails are found growing on canal banks, in the Everglades, and other swampy areas. To harvest, pull up the center stalk, the bottom is white, tender, and edible. While collecting cattails, keep an eye peeled for sleeping snakes curled up at the water's edge. Don't grope blindly. Most snake bites occur on the hands. If you see one, and you probably won't, just turn around and go the other way. After all, he lives there.

Cattail hearts
Salt and pepper
Butter

Steam or boil in a small amount of water until tender, about 10-12 minutes. Season with salt, pepper, and butter, or your favorite seasoning.

Avocado—The Shy Alligator Pear

Native to Latin America and scattered throughout Florida by Spanish explorers, avocados were called "Alligator Pears" by our pioneers.

The quaint name stems from certain types which are pear-shaped and have a rough, green skin, but avocados come in a variety of shapes and colors—some maroon, some brown, some long, and some round.

Avocados were formally introduced to South Florida in the 1830s by Dr. Henry Perrine, a physician and New York native, who became interested in tropical plants while serving as the United States Consul of the Yucatan Peninsula. He was granted land in the "lower Florida wilds," the location of today's Everglades National Park. From here, Perrine cultivated avocados as well as Key limes.

One of the oldest trees I know of dates back to the 1860s and still bears pears. It was planted by Edmond Beasley, who homesteaded the property now known as the Barnacle, a state historic site in Coconut Grove. Coincidentally, Beasley was commonly known as "Alligator Beasley," not for his love of alligator pears, but his appetite for Alligator en Brochette.

Avocado meat is the color, texture, and consistency of butter. A delicate nutty flavor makes this fruit a veritable chameleon for the creative cook. Equally compatible with sugar or salt, avocados can serve as a basic ingredient in everything from soups to sherbet. Many simply slice them for salads.

Florida has more than 100 different varieties, which are harvested from June through March. Avocados do not ripen on the tree and hide among the large lustrous leaves until picked. A shy fellow, the avocado prefers to ripen in the privacy of a small paper bag. Check him daily. When he yields to a gentle squeeze, he is ready, and you'll find that his skin pulls away easily.

Sliced avocados, like apples, will darken with exposure to air. Prevent this by covering with a thin layer of mayonnaise, a sprinkling of lime juice, or leave the seed in the pear and cover with plastic wrap.

Avocados are high in potassium, which helps regulate heart rhythm and muscle contraction. They're also high in calories, yielding about ninety-six calories to a half-cup serving.

As a snack, I eat the alligator pear cupped in my hand, halved, unpeeled, cantalope-like, with a spoon. To counteract the high caloric count of this delicacy, wash it in lime juice and eat it standing up. Surely standing takes more energy, and of course, it's common knowledge that cutting into anything allows all the calories to fall out.

Growing Your Own Tree

1. Gently wash the seed in warm water.
2. With the seed pointy end up, insert three toothpicks horizontally about midway into the sides and suspend the skewered seed over a jar. Fill the jar with water high enough to cover the bottom half inch of the seed.

3.   Place on a window sill. Change or replenish water as needed. The seed will crack and usually sprout within seven weeks.

4.   When the plant reaches a height of about fifteen inches, cut off the top three inches to create a multi-branched tree. Without this treatment you will end up with a thirty foot tree resembling a Norfolk Island Pine. I know, I have one.

5.   After the new growth appears, plant it in an eight to ten-inch pot with good drainage. Lightly fertilize about every three weeks. Eventually, if you are lucky enough to live in South Florida, you can move it into your yard and harvest the fruit of your labor.

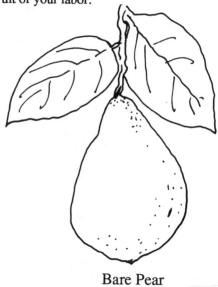

Bare Pear

Serves 2

1   avocado
1   Key lime
2   spoons

Cut the pear in half lengthwise. Remove seed. "Bathe" in lime juice. Eat out of hand. It's great picnic fare.

Shrimp Salad

Serves 6

3 1/2   cups shrimp, cooked (see recipe for Shrimp Basics), peeled, deveined and cut into bite size pieces
1   cup celery, chopped
1/3   cup onion, finely chopped
1   cup green pepper, chopped

1/4   cup fresh lime juice
2   hard boiled eggs, chopped
2   tablespoons catsup
2   teaspoons sugar
1 1/2   teaspoons vinegar
1   teaspoon Worcestershire sauce
1/2   teaspoon salt
1   teaspoon Tabasco sauce or to taste
3/4   cup re*al* mayonnaise (not salad dressing)

1.   In a 2-quart mixing bowl combine: shrimp, celery, eggs, green pepper, onion, and pour lime juice over all.
2.   In a small bowl combine all remaining ingredients, except mayonnaise. Pour over shrimp and stir in.
3.   Add mayonnaise, blend well. Chill, serve on lettuce.

Lobster Salad

Same as above but substitute cooked lobster for shrimp.

Marinated Conch Salad

Yield 3 cups or 6-8 servings

It is said by Bahamians that conch contains an aphrodisiac.

1   cup ground raw conch (1/2 pound or about 3 conch)
1/2 cup lime juice, fresh squeezed
1/2 cup onion, finely chopped
2/3 cup green pepper, finely chopped
1/2 cup celery, finely chopped
1   cup tomato, chopped
1   clove garlic, minced
1/4 cup olive oil
2   teaspoons parsley
1/4 teaspoon oregano
1/8 teaspoon curry powder
1/2 teaspoon salt
1   teaspoon Worcestershire sauce
1   teaspoon or more Tabasco sauce (to taste)

Combine all ingredients, refrigerate. Marinate at least four hours. Serve chilled with crackers.

Lime Jello Salad

6-8 generous servings

This jello salad may be left at room temperature for long periods of time and will not melt or lose its shape. It's delicious too. Tastes like Key lime pie.

6   ounce package lime jello
1   cup boiling water
8   ounce package cream cheese (room temperature)
20 ounce can crushed pineapple in own juice
1   cup broken walnuts
1/2 cup mayonnaise

1. Melt jello in boiling water, stirring until dissolved. Mash cream cheese into this liquid, blending as well as you can. It will be lumpy.
2. Stir in remaining ingredients, including the pineapple juice.
3. Pour into 2-quart bowl or jello mold. Refrigerate 3 hours.
4. Remove mold and serve cold.

Almond Chicken With Grapes

Serves 6

This recipe is even better the second day when flavors have had a chance to blend.

1   whole chicken
1/4   cup fresh lime juice (about 2 limes)
1 1/2   cups celery, chopped (about 3 ribs)
1-2   cups seedless grapes
2 1/4   ounce package almonds, sliced
2-4   tablespoons capers, crushed
Mayonnaise—about 1/2 cup (not salad dressing)
Salt and pepper to taste

1. Place the chicken in a large pot, almost covering with water. Bring to a boil, cover with lid, and turn heat to medium or low. Let cook for 1 hour or until chicken almost falls from bone. Let chicken cool, then strip meat from bones and place meat in a large bowl. Discard skin or use in Tail Waggin' Dog Soup recipe.
2. Add all remaining ingredients and enough mayonnaise to bind it all together.
3. Refrigerate, serve cold on a bed of lettuce.

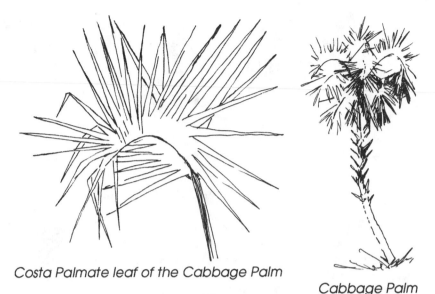

Costa Palmate leaf of the Cabbage Palm

Cabbage Palm

Cedar Key Heart of Palm Salad

Serves 4

Anyone who has ever been to Cedar Key has probably had its famous Heart of Palm Salad with Bessie Gibb's outrageous dressing.

The Salad

Torn lettuce
Heart of Palm, sliced thin
Pineapple chunks
Dried apricot or peach pieces
Chopped dates

Prepare 4 separate salad bowls with the above ingredients.

Carol Garvin's Version of Bessie Gibb's Original Peanut Butter Dressing

3	tablespoons crunchy peanut butter
1 1/2	tablespoons mayonnaise (not salad dressing)
6	tablespoons vanilla ice cream

Whisper of ginger
Green food coloring (optional)

Soften ice cream, blend in all ingredients and enough food coloring to give a pale green color. Refreeze. Place about 1 ounce in the center of each salad just before serving.

Spanish Cob Coin, piece of four—equivalent to twenty-five cents

Granny Snell's Cool Cucumber Salad

Serves 4-6

This brings back warm memories of days spent "treasure" diving off the Florida Keys with Grandpa Snell. Late afternoon, sunburned, tuckered out, and famished we would all descend on Granny. After we showered and changed, Granny would assemble us all at a large picnic table in the lacy shade of a huge poinciana tree. There we would feast like royalty on her wonderful home cooking, washing it all down with huge pitchers of Key limeade.

2	large cucumbers, sliced—or 6 cups
2	cups onion, sliced
3	cups cider vinegar
1	cup sugar
1/2	cup water

Peeling cucumbers is optional. Slice cucumbers and onions. Dissolve sugar in vinegar and water. Pour over cucumbers. Serve cold. (More onions and cucumbers can be added to vinegar mixture later.)

One Penny Can't Jingle*
(Mixed Veggie Salad)

Serves 6

*This is eastern Caribbean vernacular for "it takes two to tango."

16	ounce package mixed frozen vegetables without onions
1/2	cup onion, finely chopped
1	cup celery, finely chopped
8	ounce can sliced water chestnuts, drained

Salt and pepper
Miracle Whip

1.   Cook vegetables according to directions on package, do not over-cook. They must be crisp.
2.   Combine onion, celery, chestnuts, and vegetables. Season. Carefully fold in enough Miracle Whip to bind it all together. Serve cold.

Tom Wile's Spinach Salad

Serves 6-8

Tom is a wonderful friend and veterinarian. He has nursed my canine family through one crisis after another. Notice the "Sweets" chapter heading illustration. Every dog there, was a patient of Tom's.

The Salad

1   package fresh spinach
1   can sliced water chestnuts, drained
1   can bean sprouts, drained
3   hard boiled eggs, chopped
Crumbled bacon

Clean spinach by agitating greens in a large bowl of water. Sand sinks to the bottom. It usually requires 3 washings. Tear up greens, mix all ingredients except egg and bacon. Use these on top.

The Dressing (Sweet and Sour)

1/2-3/4   cup sugar
1/3   cup catsup
1   cup oil
1/4   cup vinegar
2   teaspoons Worcestershire sauce
1   tablespoon onion, grated

Combine all ingredients in a jar with a lid. Cap. Shake well. Serve on spinach salad.

Palmate Leaf

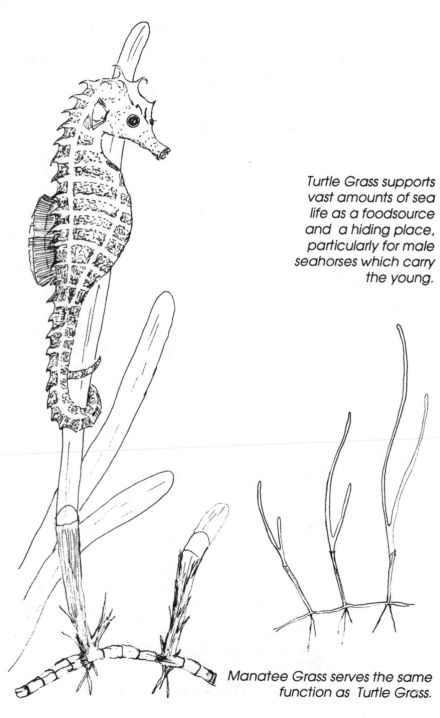

Turtle Grass supports
vast amounts of sea
life as a foodsource
and a hiding place,
particularly for male
seahorses which carry
the young.

Manatee Grass serves the same
function as Turtle Grass.

Hodge Podge Caesar Salad

Serves 5
(Because that is how many
are in the Kuhl family)

Matt Kuhl, my sixteen-year-old partner at art shows, shared his secret recipe with me. I copied it exactly, because Matt is so precise.

1	head romaine lettuce, washed
3	large toes of garlic
4	egg yolks (use the whites for Becky's Mud Puppy Mousse recipe)
3/4	cup corn oil
2	tablespoons teriyaki sauce
1	tablespoon Worcestershire sauce
2	dashes Tabasco
1	tablespoon soy sauce
2	teaspoons lemon juice
1	tablespoon red wine
3/4	teaspoon mustard

Pepper to taste
1/4   cup grated Parmesan cheese
Croutons
Salad Topping

In a slope-sided wooden bowl, squeeze garlic through a press. With a wooden spoon, grind the garlic's oil so as to cover the bottom of the bowl. Remove pulp. Mix all the yolks in. While stirring vigorously and continuously in small circles, pour in the oil *very, very* slowly. Then add the teriyaki, Worcestershire sauce, Tabasco, soy sauce, lemon juice, wine, mustard, pepper, and parmesan cheese, adjusting to taste. Mix well. Fold in lettuce. Throw on croutons and salad topping.

The Florida Scrub Jay breeds only in the piney woods; has a blue head, tail, and wings, light gray belly, and tan back.

Finishing Touches—
Sweets

Coconut Palm (Cocos nucifera)

This useful tree has been spread throughout the tropics by man and sea to such a degree that its original home is a mystery.

Outranked only by grasses in economic importance, the entire tree can be used in one way or another. The coconut not only yields food products and cosmetics, but charcoal, rope products, woven items, medicine, fertilizer, dyes, and much more. During World War II, when glucose was in short supply in the Pacific Islands, coconut water, which is sterile within the nut and contains a natural sugar, was used as an intravenous substitute.

The majestic coconut palms have flowers and nuts in all stages of development, yielding coconuts all year long, about seventy-five annually. It takes about one full year from flower to mature nut, seven years for the tree to produce its first nuts, and another eight years to fully mature. For the next fifty years the palm will be at peak production; then with the onset of old age, it gradually produces less and less. Finally, old unproductive trees are cut down, yielding a beautiful hardwood commonly called porcupine wood, which is so heavy it sinks in water.

Immature nuts are sometimes called ice cream coconuts, because the meat has a jelly-like consistency. As the nut matures, the meat absorbs the water and becomes firm. Inside the nut, beneath the soft eye, is a single tiny seed. Out of this eye will come the green sprout and roots, eventually pushing out through the husk. If left undisturbed, the water and meat develop into a spongy tissue called "uto" by South Sea islanders. The uto nourishes the sprouting nut, and remarkably, even at this stage, it may be sliced, toasted, and eaten.

Growing bananas and coconuts together is a common practice in the islands. Bananas produce and die off quickly, and the decaying banana stalks provide the nutrients necessary for the coconut palm to thrive.

Finding the Right Nut

Shake the nut to see how much water it contains—the more the better. Green or drinking nuts picked from the tree will be heavy. Shaking them produces no sound, as they are completely full of liquid. I like green nuts for pies because the meat is less firm. Mature nuts are crunchy.

The Horseshoe Crab hasn't changed in 200 million years, has four eyes, and contains some edible muscle considered a delicacy.

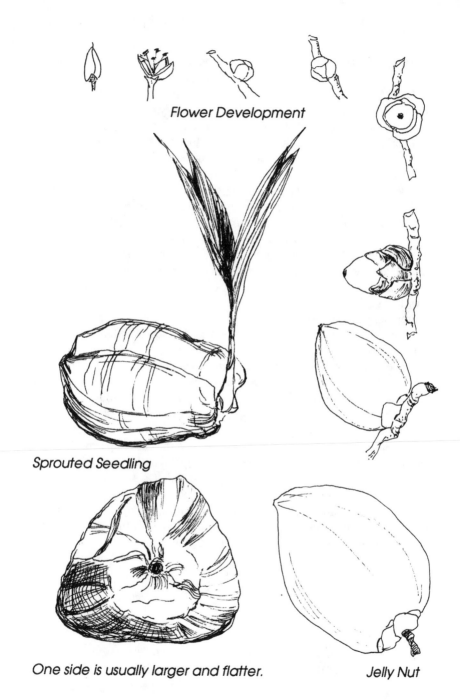

Flower Development

Sprouted Seedling

One side is usually larger and flatter.

Jelly Nut

Tackling the Nut

The easiest way to husk a coconut is to buy one already denuded at the store. But if you're the pioneering type and want to burn a few calories, here are a few hints:

1. Designate a husking area.

2. Assemble tools of your choice: hammer and chisel, machete, or sharp stick driven into the ground.

3. Provide ear plugs for spectators who abhor blue language.

4. Have a First aid kit handy. (This procedure has been known to draw blood.)

Split the husk by pounding the nut on a sharp stick, or use a hammer and chisel or machete. I prefer the hammer and chisel. I've been using this method since I was seven years old; it's slow but painless.

El Coco (The Monkey Face)

Assuming all went well with the husking, you now have a naked nut. Turn him so you're looking his monkey face straight in the eyes. Cuban legend calls this face "El Coco," their bogie man. Punch out the eyes with a nail or ice pick. Drain the water into a glass and taste it. If the water is good, so is the nut.

For ease in removing the meat from the shell, micro- wave it for one minute on high or bake it at 300° F for ten minutes. Then lightly tap your nut all over with a hammer to loosen the meat. If you want to save the shell for a bowl, tap lightly but firmly around the nut where you want it to break, until it comes apart in two halves. You can saw it for a smoother edge but that's work. Carefully pry out the meat with a round-tipped table knife. Rinse the meat. Trimming off brown skin is optional; I don't bother.

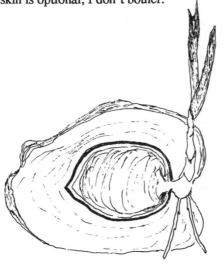

*Cut away showing
the sprouted nut.*

Coconut Water, Milk, Cream, and Butter

Water is the liquid in the nut.

For Milk—Blenderize or grate coconut as fine as possible. Line a bowl with a cloth and pour 1 cup hot tap water over 1 cup of blenderized nut. Gather the edges of the cloth and twist to extract as much liquid as possible. (For a richer blend use hot milk.)

For Cream—Make coconut milk and set aside, cream will rise to the top. Skim it off and use it as a rich dairy cream.

For Butter—Beat the chilled cream with a mixer until butter forms. Press out water and season with salt if desired. Refrigerate.

Measures and Nutritional Information

The average coconut weighs 1 1/2 lbs. and yields 3-4 cups of meat.
1 oz. = 4 tbs. grated meat
1 oz. = 175 calories
Coconut oil is high in saturated fat.

Fresh Coconut Cake

Serves 10

This is my Mother's recipe. It's everything you always thought a coconut cake should be.

2/3	cup margarine
1 3/4	cups sugar
3	cups cake flour*
1	tablespoon plus 1/2 teaspoon baking powder
3/4	teaspoon salt
Whisper of ginger	
1 1/3	cups milk
2	teaspoons vanilla
3	large eggs, separated
1/2	cup fresh grated coconut or 1/2 cup shredded commercially prepared coconut

1. Preheat oven to 350° F. Grease 3 8" round cake pans.
2. In a large mixing bowl with an electric mixer, cream margarine and sugar until light and fluffy. Mixture will be lemon colored. Add yolks and blend well.
3. Sift together, salt, flour, baking powder, and ginger. Add alternately with milk to above mixture. Blend well after each addition. Add vanilla, blend well. Set aside.
4. Wash beaters in hot soapy water. Making sure bowl and beaters are absolutely grease-free, whip the egg whites until stiff. Fold egg whites and coconut into batter. Pour into cake pans.
5. Bake about 30 minutes, toothpick inserted should come out clean. Cool completely. Frost with Coconut Frosting (recipe to follow).

*If you don't have store-bought cake flour, here's the substitute.

Cake Flour

1. Put 2 level tablespoons corn starch into a measuring cup.
2. Fill to 1 cup mark with all purpose flour.
3. Sift 3 times. Makes 1 cup cake flour.

Coconut Frosting

1/4 cup flour
1   cup milk
1   cup margarine or shortening*
1   cup sugar
1   teaspoon vanilla
Juice of one calamondin or 2 teaspoons fresh lemon juice (optional)
2   cups fresh grated coconut or 2 cups commercially prepared shredded coconut

1. Sift flour into saucepan, slowly add milk, stirring constantly until all milk is absorbed and mixture is smooth. Cook over medium-low heat stirring constantly until very thick. Set aside to cool.
2. In a mixing bowl, beat sugar and shortening or margarine at high speed until light and fluffy. Blend in flavorings. Add cold flour mixture, beat until frosting stands up in stiff peaks. This cannot be over beaten.
3. Fold in one cup coconut. Frost cake. Sprinkle or pat remaining coconut on sides and top of cake. Wow! It tastes as great as it looks.

*Margarine will give the frosting a cream-color while shortening is a pure white color.

Carrot Cake

Yields 12 snacks

A moist, spicy cake. And good breakfast food to take on sailing trips.

2	cups canned carrots (a little less than 2 16 ounce cans)
2	cups sugar
1	cup oil
4	large eggs
2	teaspoons baking soda
1	tablespoon baking powder
1/2	teaspoon salt
2	teaspoons cinnamon
1/4	teaspoon each nutmeg and cloves
1/8	teaspoon each ginger and allspice
1	teaspoon vanilla
3	cups sifted flour
1/2	cup broken walnuts
1/2	cup raisins

1. Preheat oven to 350° F. Grease tube or bundt pan.
2. Drain carrots, mash, and drain again. Measure 2 cups, packing carrots in measuring cup.
3. In a large mixing bowl, combine all ingredients, beat well with an electric mixer. Pour into tube pan.
4. Bake for 1 1/4 hours or until toothpick inserted comes out clean. Top with Vanilla Glaze.

Vanilla Glaze

2	cups sifted confectioners sugar
2	tablespoons softened margarine
1	teaspoon vanilla
Milk	

In a small bowl, combine all ingredients, add milk a few drops at a time; glaze will have a thin, spreadable consistency. Spread over top of slightly warm cake. It will drizzle down the sides.

Glazed Key Lime Pound Cake

Serves 10

1   box lemon cake with pudding in the mix
1/2 cup fresh lime juice
1/3 cup oil
2   tablespoons water
1/2 cup plain yogurt
4   eggs

1.   Disregard all instructions on the cake mix box. Preheat oven to 350° F.
2.   Combine all ingredients in a large mixing bowl. Beat at high speed for 2-3 minutes, until smooth and well-blended.
3.   Pour into a well-greased tube pan. Bake 40-45 minutes. Top of cake does not turn brown, but toothpick inserted comes out clean. While cake is still warm *carefully* remove from pan.

Lime Glaze

1/3 cup fresh lime juice
2   cups sifted confectioners sugar

Mix above ingredients, pour over warm cake.

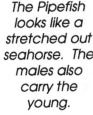

The Pipefish looks like a stretched out seahorse. The males also carry the young.

Cape Florida Lighthouse, circa 1825

Blind Tiger
(Orange Cake)

Old-timers sometimes called moonshine "Blind Tiger." This orange cake contains quite a bit of liquor, hence the name.

1	cup (2 sticks) margarine, softened
1	cup sugar
4	eggs, separated
1	tablespoon grated orange rind*
1/4	cup frozen orange juice concentrate, undiluted
3/4	cup sour cream
1 3/4	cups flour
1	teaspoon baking powder
1	teaspoon baking soda
1/2	teaspoon nutmeg

Whisper of salt

1. Preheat oven to 325° F.
2. In a large mixing bowl cream margarine and sugar. Add orange rind, egg yolks, orange concentrate, and sour cream.
3. Sift together dry ingredients. Blend into above mixture.
4. Beat egg whites until stiff. Fold into batter.
5. Pour into greased tube pan. Bake 1 hour or until toothpick inserted comes out clean. Read on so you will be ready.

*Grate off orange surface skin only. Avoid white skin below. It's bitter.

Orange Syrup et. al.

3/4	cup sugar
1/2	cup frozen orange juice concentrate, undiluted
1/8	teaspoon salt
1/2-2/3	cup Triple Sec—set aside
1/2	cup chopped pecans—set aside

1. Combine first 3 ingredients in a sauce pan. Boil about 4 minutes.
2. Let cake cool 10 minutes, then turn out onto cake plate. With a fork, liberally perforate top of cake. Then slowly, slowly, pour on Triple Sec, so it is absorbed into the cake. Then equally slowly spoon on syrup. Top with broken pecans.

Calamondin Cake

Serves 10

1	cup margarine, softened
2 1/2	cups sugar
5	eggs
1	cup mandarin orange yogurt
1/2	cup milk
1/4	teaspoon salt
3 1/2	teaspoons baking powder
1	teaspoon baking soda
3	cups flour
1/2	cup pureed calamondins with peel—no seeds

1. Preheat oven to 325° F.
2. In a large mixing bowl, cream margarine and sugar. Add eggs, beat well. Add remaining ingredients, beat vigorously until well blended. Pour into greased 9 x 13 inch pan.
3. Bake 50-60 minutes or until toothpick inserted comes out clean.
4. Frost with Fudgy Frosting if you like the mix of orange and chocolate. If not, use the Cream Cheese Frosting recipe or the Sour Cream Frosting.

Fudgy Frosting

1/2 cup margarine
1/3 cup white corn syrup
1/4 teaspoon salt
1/2 teaspoon vanilla
1/2 cup powdered cocoa
3 cups confectioners sugar, sifted
2 tablespoons milk

Using electric mixer, cream margarine in a medium sized bowl. Add corn syrup, salt, and vanilla. Blend well. Add in cocoa and powdered sugar, blend. Slowly add milk until frosting reaches a spreadable consistency. You may need more milk. Spread on cool cake.

Or

Sour Cream Frosting

2 cups sugar
1 cup sour cream
1/2 cup chopped nuts
1 teaspoon vanilla

Combine sugar and sour cream. Boil over low heat until a bit dropped into cold water forms a soft ball (a slightly flattened shape). Remove from heat. Cool till lukewarm. Beat with a mixer until creamy. Add nuts and vanilla. Spread immediately.

Cinderella Cake
(Pumpkin Cake)

Serves 12

2   cups cooked or canned pumpkin
4   eggs
1   cup oil
2   cups flour
2   teaspoons baking soda
2   teaspoons cinnamon
1/2 teaspoon salt
1   tablespoon baking powder
1/4 teaspoon nutmeg
1/4 teaspoon cloves
1/4 teaspoon allspice
1/4 teaspoon ginger

1.   Preheat oven to 350° F.
2.   Combine all ingredients in a large mixing bowl. Blend well. Pour into a well-greased 9 x 13 inch pan. Bake 35-40 minutes or until toothpick inserted comes out clean. Cool.

Cream Cheese Frosting

1/2 cup margarine
1   box confectioners sugar
8   ounce package softened cream cheese
2   teaspoons vanilla
Whisper of ginger
1/2 cup broken pecans or walnuts

Using a mixer, combine all ingredients except nuts. Blend well. Frost cooled cake. Top with nuts.

Dutch Belted Cows were a common sight at the White Belt Dairy in Miami during the 1950s and 1960s. Their curious but uniform coloration (black fore and aft with a white band in the middle) made the cows appear painted.

100 Year Old Gingerbread Recipe

Serves 10

1/2	cup margarine (1 stick)
1/2	cup sugar
1	teaspoon vanilla
1	large egg
2 1/2	cups sifted flour
1 1/2	teaspoons baking soda
1	heaping teaspoon cinnamon
1/2	teaspoon ginger
1/4	teaspoon each, cloves, nutmeg, and allspice
1/2	teaspoon salt
1	cup molasses
1	cup hot water

1. Preheat oven to 350° F. Grease 8 inch or 9 inch square pan.
2. In a large mixing bowl with an electric mixer, cream margarine, sugar, and vanilla. Add egg, mix well.
3. Mix molasses with hot water. Add to above mixture alternately with dry ingredients. Blend well between each addition.
4. Bake for about 45 minutes or until toothpick inserted in center comes out clean.
5. Serve warm, plain or topped with Lemon Sauce or vanilla ice cream.

Lemon Sauce

1	lemon, juice and peel
6	tablespoons real butter, *no substitutes*
1/2	cup sugar
1 1/4	cups water
Whisper of salt	
2	tablespoons cornstarch

1. Grate peel off lemon, juice lemon. Stir cornstarch into lemon juice.
2. In a small sauce pan over medium-low heat melt butter, then add sugar. Stir until well blended. Add remaining ingredients except cornstarch/lemon juice mixture, blend, then add cornstarch mixture, stirring constantly until thickened. You may raise the temperature to medium to hasten the thickening process, but don't go wandering off, stay by your pot.
3. Serve warm over gingerbread.

Old Fashioned Rose Geranium Cake

Yields 10 servings

This is a type of geranium with a very fuzzy leaf and a delightful "Rosy" scent which through baking imparts a very delicate flavor in the cake.

1 cup margarine
2 cups sugar
4 eggs
3 cups flour
2 teaspoons baking powder
1/3 cup milk
2/3 cup sour cream
1 teaspoon vanilla
Rose geranium leaves
Powdered sugar

1. Preheat oven to 350° F.
2. Cream margarine and sugar. Add eggs, beat well. Alternate dry and liquid ingredients.
3. Grease tube pan. Line entire pan with leaves. Most of the scent dissipates so use lots. Carefully pour in batter.
4. Bake for 1 hour or until toothpick inserted comes out clean.
5. Cool for 15 minutes. Remove from pan. When completely cool, sift powdered sugar on top.

Darkest Devil's Food Cake

Serves 10

1 3/4 cups sifted flour
1 3/4 cups sugar
3/4 cup Hershey's powdered cocoa
2 teaspoons baking soda
1 teaspoon baking powder
1 teaspoon salt
3 tablespoons instant coffee
2 large eggs
1/2 cup oil
1 cup water
1 cup plain yogurt
1 teaspoon vanilla

1. Preheat oven to 350° F. Grease 9 x 13 x 2 inch rectangular pan.
2. In a large mixing bowl, combine all dry ingredients. Blend well.
3. Add remaining ingredients, beat vigorously with electric mixer, until smooth. This batter is soupier than usual. Pour into pan. Bake 35-40 minutes or until toothpick inserted into center comes out clean. Do not remove from pan.

Spicy Chocolate Frosting

1/2 box confectioners sugar sifted (1 pound box)
6 tablespoons Hershey's powdered cocoa
Whisper each—salt, ginger, cinnamon
5 tablespoons margarine, softened
1 teaspoon vanilla
2-4 tablespoons milk or enough to make frosting smooth and
spreadable

1. Sift all dry ingredients together. Beat in margarine and vanilla.
2. Add milk, 1 tablespoon at a time, until frosting becomes smooth and spreadable. Spread on warm cake. Serve.

See Magic Mint Icing for alternate icing

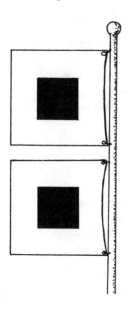

Hurricane Warning Flag

Black Magic
(Chocolate Cake)

2	cups sifted flour
1 3/4	cups sugar
3/4	cup Hershey's Powdered Cocoa
2 1/4	teaspoons baking soda
1 1/4	teaspoons baking powder
1	teaspoon salt
3	tablespoons instant coffee
3	large eggs
1/2	cup oil
1	cup water
1	cup mashed avocado
1	teaspoon vanilla

Portuguese Man of War

1. Preheat oven to 350° F.
2. In a large mixing bowl combine all dry ingredients. Blend well.
3. Add remaining ingredients. Beat vigorously with an electric mixer until well blended.
4. Pour into well-greased tube pan. Bake 50-60 minutes or until toothpick inserted comes out clean.

Magic Mint Icing

Part I

1/2 cup margarine or butter, softened
3 cups sifted confectioners sugar
3 tablespoons creme de menthe

Combine all ingredients. Blend with electric mixer until smooth. Spread on cool cake. Refrigerate.

Part II

2 ounces semi-sweet baking chocolate
2 tablespoons margarine
1 tablespoon light corn syrup

1. Melt chocolate and margarine over low heat, stirring constantly. Add corn syrup. Stir until smooth.
2. Drizzle over mint icing.

Island Decadence
(Rum Cake)

1 3/4	cups sifted flour
1 3/4	cups sugar
3/4	cup Hershey's powdered cocoa
2	teaspoons baking soda
2	teaspoons baking powder
1	teaspoon salt
3	tablespoons instant coffee
3	large eggs
1/2	cup oil
1	cup sour cream
1/2	cup water
1/2	cup Triple Sec

1. Preheat oven to 325° F.
2. Combine all dry ingredients in a large mixing bowl. Blend well.
3. Add remaining ingredients, beat vigorously with an electric mixer until well blended.
4. Pour into a well-greased tube pan. Bake 50-60 minutes or until toothpick inserted comes out clean. Carefully remove from pan while still warm.

Soak and Glaze

Soak
2/3	cup rum

Poke holes with a two-tined kitchen fork all over top of cake. Pour 2/3 cup rum *slowly* into cake until it is all absorbed.

Glaze
2	cups confectioners sugar, sifted
1 1/2	tablespoons melted margarine
1/4	cup rum
1/2	cup broken pecans

Combine first 3 ingredients in order given. Spread over slightly warm cake. Spread to top edges of cake so it will spill down the sides. Top with pecans. Cover with cake lid so rum can saturate the cake.

Mi-am-uh Chocolate Cupcakes

Yields 2 dozen

Anyone who is a native Miamian of the post-World War II era will fondly remember these cupcakes. They were chocolate cake with vanilla creme filling and chocolate icing. Holsum Bakery made them, six to a box. I don't know why they ever stopped. They were wonderful.

1   box Pillsbury Plus Devil's Food Cake Mix or Betty Crocker Super Moist Devil's Food Cake Mix
1   box cupcake papers (optional)

Prepare cake mix as directed on box. Make 24 cupcakes. Allow to cool.

Vanilla Creme Filling

1 1/2   cups confectioners sugar, sifted
1/2   cup margarine, softened
1/4   cup water
2   teaspoons vanilla

1.   Combine all ingredients. Beat with electric mixer until fluffy.
2.   Fill cake decorating bag with large diameter metal tip with vanilla creme. Insert tip into top of cupcake and squeeze in filling.

The Snowy Egret is a member of the Heron family which flies with head reefed in.

Chocolate Frosting
1 can (16 ounce) Betty Crocker Creamy Deluxe Chocolate Frosting or
(16 ounce) Pillsbury Chocolate Fudge or (16 ounce) Pillsbury Chocolate Funfetti—chocolate icing with colored sugar sprinkles

Spread over cupcakes.

Bald cypress shed their needles in winter. As the needles decay and become acidic, the limestone beneath the trees dissolves, forming ponds which support a myriad of wildlife.

Chocolate Cheese Cake Extraordinaire

Serves 10

Walnut Crust

1 1/2   cups crushed walnuts
2   tablespoons sugar
2   tablespoons softened margarine

1. Preheat oven to 400° F.
2. In a mixing bowl blend all ingredients well. Press into 8 or 9 inch pie plate.
3. Bake 6 minutes or until golden.

Cheese Cake

6   squares (6 ounces) semi sweet baking chocolate
1   pound cream cheese (2 eight ounce packages)
1/2   cup sugar
2   large eggs
1   teaspoon vanilla
2/3   cup mandarin orange yogurt

1. Reduce oven heat to 275° F.
2. Over low heat or in a microwave melt chocolate.
3. In a mixing bowl beat cream cheese and sugar until smooth. Beat in eggs and vanilla. Blend chocolate and yogurt into mixture.
4. Pour into crust. Bake 1 hour 15 minutes. Cool and refrigerate.

Topping For Chocolate Cheese Cake

1/2 pint heavy whipping cream
2   tablespoons confectioners sugar

1. Chill bowl and beaters in freezer 15 minutes.
2. Pour whipping cream into bowl whip until thick. Add sugar. Then whip until stiff.
3. Spread on cold cheesecake. Store in refrigerator.

Avocado Amaretto Cheese Cake

Serves 10

Crust for a 9 inch pie plate
2/3 or more cup sliced almonds, toasted
1/3 cup graham cracker crumbs
3   tablespoons margarine, melted
1/4 cup sugar

Cheese Cake
1/4 cup Amaretto
1/2 cup almond paste
1/2 cup avocado, mashed
12 ounces cream cheese (1 1/2 eight ounce packages), softened
1/3 cup sugar
1 tablespoon flour
2 eggs
1/2 cup almond slices

Topping
1 cup sour cream
3 tablespoons Amaretto
2 tablespoons sugar
1/4 cup toasted almonds

Crust
1. Preheat oven to 350° F.
2. Pour sliced almonds into a baggie. Crush almonds by squeezing baggie. Measure 2/3 cup. Pour into a small flat pan, toast for about 5 minutes or until golden.
3. Melt margarine. Mix toasted almonds, Graham cracker crumbs, and sugar. Pat into a 9 inch pie pan. Bake 5 minutes. Set aside.

Cake
1. In a large mixing bowl combine Amaretto, almond paste, avocado, and cream cheese. Blend well. Add sugar and flour. Mix well. Beat in eggs. Stir in almonds.
2. Bake for 40 minutes at 350° F.

Topping
Combine all ingredients except almonds. Spread on hot cheese cake. Sprinkle on almonds. Return to oven for 15 minutes. Serve cold from refrigerator.

The Blue Porter Weed has purple flowers with white centers and is shown at actual size.

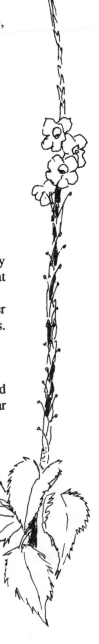

Coconut Planters' homes and surfboats.

Coconut Planters

The introduction of coconut palms to Florida, though not mysterious, is a saga of entrepreneurial dreams and disappointments.

While sailing on Biscayne Bay in 1870, Ohio nurseryman Henry Lum went ashore on an uninhabited barrier island. He found three coconut trees thriving untended, was intrigued, and bought the land for thirty-five cents an acre.

He learned erroneously that coconut trees mature in five years, producing about 365 nuts annually. Armed with these "facts," he and two partners acquired all the vacant beachfront from Jupiter Inlet to the Cape Florida Lighthouse—a total of sixty-five miles—for seventy-five cents to one dollar and twenty-five cents an acre.

A planting project began in 1881 with men, mules, surfboats, portable houses, tools, and supplies. Coconuts were brought in by boat from the Caribbean and planted in rows at twenty foot intervals from beach to bay. Houses had to be moved to new locations as each area was completed. Workers suffered from biting insects, aching joints, sunburn, and heat. Turnover was high as the men became disenchanted with the rugged, isolated, inhospitable conditions.

Several hundred thousand coconuts began sprouting, providing a wonderful dietary variation for local deer and rabbits. But the project was doomed. Harvesting was several years away, and with wild animals eating up the investments, financial problems ground the project to a halt.

In the end there was only one investor who successfully farmed his land, but not with coconuts. Seventy-year-old John Collins, a charming Quaker gentleman who spoke with 'thees' and 'thous,' planted and harvested nearly 3000 avocados. For years he and his family lived on the island with only shy crocodiles as neighbors.

And what about the coconut trees? The rabbits didn't get them all. As a final tribute to the men who brought them, they flourished for a century with their incomparable tropical beauty, only to be stricken with a progressive and fatal disease called Lethal Yellowing. Their numbers have dwindled and it's hard to find them among the skyscrapers, yet, over 100 years later, these majestic trees can still be found throughout the area, particularly on Mr. Lum's island, now called Miami Beach.

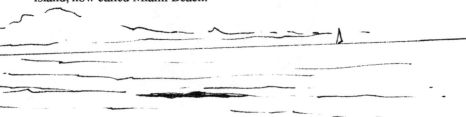

Memorable Pie Crust

A few words about pie crust ... I started using margarine in my crust to avoid the annoyance of measuring shortening. Once I tasted crust made with margarine, well that was a memorable experience. If you think margarine won't make a difference, try shortening on your toast in the morning.

One Crust

6 1/3	tablespoons margarine
1	cup sifted all purpose flour
1/2	teaspoon salt

2-2 1/2	tablespoons water

Two Crusts

3/4	cup margarine
2 1/2	cups flour
1	teaspoon salt
5	tablespoons water

1. Preheat oven to 450° F.
2. Cut margarine into salt and flour with pastry cutter until crumbly. Mix in 2 tablespoons water. Work in with your hands. If it is too dry, add enough water to give dough a nice pliable consistency.
3. Roll out between 2 pieces of well-floured waxed paper. Turn into plate. If you are baking an empty shell, prick bottom liberally with a fork.
4. Bake for 10-15 minutes or until golden, unless your recipe calls for an unbaked shell.

Green Coconut Pie

Serves 8-10

Large green coconuts picked from the tree yield a softer meat, producing a smooth textured pie. You'll know if you have the magic coconut when you pry the meat from the shell. The skin will be a pale tan instead of brown. But any coconut can be used. This pie is magnificent.

Meat from one coconut or 2 cups commercially prepared flaked coconut

1   9 inch *baked* pie crust (store-bought or see Memorable Pie Crust recipe)
1   cup sugar
1/2 cup cornstarch
1/4 teaspoon salt
3   cups milk, skim or whole
3   large egg yolks, beaten
1/2 teaspoon almond extract
1   teaspoon vanilla extract
2   cups heavy whipping cream

1.   In a food processor or blender, grind up the fresh coconut as fine as possible. I do not pare off the brown skin on the outside of the nut, but you may if you wish.
2.   In a two quart sauce pan, combine sugar, cornstarch and salt. Stir until well blended. Add milk slowly, stirring until smooth. Cook over medium heat, stirring constantly until mixture boils and begins to thicken. Remove from heat. Remove a small amount of mixture (about 1 cup) from the pan and slowly stir into egg yolks. When well blended, pour into sauce pan, return to heat, and continue cooking until the custard is thick enough to "mound" on the spoon.
3.   Remove from heat, stir in extracts and all coconut, reserving a handful for top of pie. Pour into a bowl and cover with waxed paper laid directly on the custard. Refrigerate to completely chill, about 3 hours.
4.   Three hours later, chill bowl and beaters for 15 minutes in freezer. Whip heavy cream in chilled bowl with electric mixer until stiff. Fold 3/4 whipped cream into custard.
5.   Pour into pie shell. Spread remaining whipped cream on top. Sprinkle coconut on top. Refrigerate 3 hours before serving. Store in the refrigerator.

Black Bottom Coconut Lime Pie

Serves 8

1   9 inch *baked* pie crust, completely cooled (store-bought or see Memorable
Pie Crust recipe)
2   ounces semi-sweet baking chocolate
4   eggs, separated
1/4   cup plus 1 tablespoon fresh Key lime juice
1   tablespoon grated lime peel*
2   tablespoons water
1   cup sugar
Coconut (freshly grated or commercially prepared shredded)

1.   Melt chocolate and spread over bottom of *baked* pie crust, sprinkle coconut on top. Preheat oven to 325° F.
2.   Separate eggs and transfer yolks into sauce pan or top of double boiler. With electric mixer beat yolks until thick and lemon colored. Stir in lime juice and water. Add 1/2 cup sugar and peel, cook over medium heat or in double boiler stirring constantly, until thick. Remove from heat.
3.   Making sure beaters and bowl are grease free, beat egg whites until foamy and add remaining 1/2 cup sugar. Beat until egg whites form stiff peaks.
4.   Fold 1/2 this mixture into lime mixture. Spoon into *baked* pie shell, spread remaining meringue on top, sprinkle with coconut.
5.   Bake 10-15 minutes or until coconut and meringue are golden.
6.   Serve cold, store in refrigerator.

*Grate peel by gently scraping off the smooth yellow or green surface skin only. Avoid the white skin below. It's bitter.

Sea Oats

Traditional Key Lime Pie

This is my mom's recipe. The whipped cream folded in has always been her secret weapon for a perfect pie.

8   inch *baked* pie crust, completely cooled (store-bought or see Memorable Pie Crust recipe)
1   can sweetened condensed milk* (14 ounces)
2   egg yolks, slightly beaten—no egg whites, they cause runny pies
1/2 cup fresh lime juice
1   tablespoon grated lime rind
1/2 pint heavy whipping cream

1.   Place a small bowl and electric beaters in freezer to chill (about 10-15 minutes).
2.   Grate rind off limes before squeezing them. Juice limes.
3.   In a medium-sized mixing bowl, combine condensed milk, juice, rind, and egg yolks, blend well. Set aside.
4.   Pour heavy cream into chilled bowl, whip with chilled beaters until stiff. Fold 1/2 to 2/3 of the whipped cream into the lime mixture. Pour into *baked* pie crust. Spread remaining whipped cream on top of pie. Refrigerate 3 hours before serving. Store in refrigerator. This is the only Key Lime Pie which is consistently firm and never runny.

*If you are without canned sweetened condensed milk, here's an emergency substitute.

Homemade Sweetened Condensed Milk

Yields about 1 1/4 cups equal to a 14 ounce can

1   cup instant non-fat dry milk solids
2/3 cup sugar
1/3 cup boiling water
3   tablespoons melted margarine

1.   Combine all ingredients in a blender. Blenderize until smooth.
2.   Refrigerate. It has to be *cold* to thicken properly.

Sand Dollar Pie

1   9 inch *baked* pie crust or 9 inch graham cracker crust (store-bought or see Memorable Pie Crust recipe)
15   ounce can sweetened condensed milk
1/2   cup Key lime juice
1/2   teaspoon grated lime rind
20   ounce can crushed pineapple, *well drained*
1   cup chopped nuts
1   cup heavy whipping cream

1.   To insure heavy cream whips properly, chill beaters and deep bowl in the freezer.
2.   In a large mixing bowl combine condensed milk, lime juice, rind, pineapple, and nuts. Chill in ice box 1 hour.
3.   Whip cream until stiff. Be careful, don't over do and end up with butter. Fold 1/2 whipped cream into pie mixture. Pour into baked pie shell.   Chill 1/2 hour.
4.   Top with remaining whipped cream. Chill 4 hours before serving.

Pecan Pie

Serves 8

1   9 inch *unbaked* pie crust (store-bought or see Memorable Pie Crust recipe)
3   eggs
1/2   teaspoon salt
1/2   cup sugar
3   tablespoons melted butter or margarine
1   cup dark corn syrup
1   teaspoon vanilla
1 1/4   cups pecans

1. Preheat oven to 450° F.
2. Using an electric mixer beat eggs well, add salt and sugar, blend. Mix in remaining ingredients. Pour into *unbaked* pie shell.
3. Bake 15 minutes at 450° F, then reduce heat to 350° F and bake an additional 30 minutes. Knife inserted should come out clean. Serve with vanilla ice cream.

Pecan Pie Surprise

Serves 8

Of course the surprise is the cheese cake layer.

9 inch *unbaked* pie crust (store-bought or see Memorable Pie Crust recipe)

Cheese Cake Layer
1/4 cup sugar
8 ounce package cream cheese
2 tablespoons milk
1 tablespoon lime juice or to taste
1/2 teaspoon vanilla
1 egg

Pecan Layer
1 tablespoon melted butter or margarine
2 eggs
1/3 cup sugar
1/4 teaspoon salt
2/3 cup dark corn syrup
1 teaspoon vanilla
2/3 cup broken pecans

1. Preheat oven to 350° F.
2. Prepare Memorable Pie Crust recipe. Place crust in 9 inch pie plate, flute edges. Prick sides and bottom with fork. Bake 10 minutes. Set aside.
3. In a mixing bowl, blend sugar and cream cheese. Add milk, vanilla, and lime juice. Taste. Add more lime juice if necessary. Beat in egg. Pour into pie crust. Set aside.
4. In a large mixing bowl, beat eggs well with electric mixer. Blend in sugar, margarine, salt, corn syrup, and vanilla.
5. Sprinkle nuts on top of cheese layer. Slowly pour on above mixture. Bake 1 hour and 10 minutes or until knife inserted comes out clean.
6. Serve cold. Store in refrigerator.

Mango Praline Pie

Serves 8

1	9 inch *unbaked* pie crust (store-bought or see Memorable Pie Crust recipe)
2/3-3/4	cup sugar (depends on sweetness of mangoes)
3	tablespoons flour
4	cups ripe mangoes, peeled and sliced
1 1/2	teaspoons lime juice
1/3	cup brown sugar
1/4	cup flour
1/2	cup pecans, chopped
3	tablespoons margarine, sliced

1. Preheat oven to 400° F.
2. Combine sugar with flour. Stir in mangoes and lime juice. Set aside.
3. Combine pecans, brown sugar, and flour. Add margarine slices. Stir until crumbly.
4. Sprinkle about 1/3 of the pecan mixture into *unbaked* pie crust. Pour in mango mixture. Top with remaining pecan mixture.
5. Bake for about 35-40 minutes or until mangoes are cooked.

Mango Pie

Serves 8

Pastry for 2 crust pie, *unbaked* (store-bought or see Memorable Pie Crust recipe)

5	cups ripe mangoes, peeled and sliced
1	teaspoon lime juice
3/4	cup honey
1/4	cup flour
1/2	teaspoon cinnamon

Whisper of ginger

2	tablespoons margarine

1. Preheat oven to 425° F.
2. Mix mangoes with lime juice. Stir in remaining ingredients except margarine.
3. Pour into an *unbaked* pie shell. Lay on margarine slices. Top with second crust. Cut vents or design into top crust.
4. Bake about 30-40 minutes or until golden. Serve cool. Top with whipped cream.

Green Mango Pie

Pastry for a 2 crust pie, *unbaked* (store-bought or see Memorable Pie Crust recipe)

1	cup sugar
2	tablespoons flour
1	teaspoon cinnamon
1/2	teaspoon nutmeg
Whisper of ginger	
1/4	teaspoon salt
4	cups green mangoes, peeled and sliced thin
2	teaspoons Key lime juice
2	tablespoons margarine

1. Preheat oven to 325° F.
2. In a large mixing bowl combine dry ingredients. Stir in mangoes and lime juice.
3. Pour into an *unbaked* pie shell. Dot with margarine. Cover with top crust. Flute edges. Cut vents into crust or create a design with cuts, such as flowers or a happy face.
4. Bake 45-50 minutes or until crust is golden and mangoes cooked. This tastes like apple pie.

Native Morning Glory has lavender flowers with white centers.

Cinnamon Apple Pie

Serves 8

Pastry for a 2 crust pie, *unbaked* (store-bought or see Memorable Pie Crust recipe)

6 or 7	cups sliced apples (peeled optional)
3/4-1	cup sugar—varies with tartness of apples
2	tablespoons flour
1/4	teaspoon salt
3	tablespoons butter
3	tablespoons Red Hots (red cinnamon candies)

1. Preheat oven to 425° F.
2. Prepare apples. Unpeeled apples can be harder to eat because the skin stays intact. I never peel mine and I've never had complaints.
3. Mix apples with salt, sugar, flour, and red hots.
4. Pour into an *unbaked* 9 inch pie shell. Dot with butter. Roll out second crust and lay on top. Flute edges and cut steam vents in the top. I usually cut something artistic—a simple daisy, a sailboat, a happy face, depending upon who is coming to dinner.
5. Bake 50-60 minutes or until crust is golden brown and juice is bubbling out of vents.

Confederate Pie
(Sweet Potato Pie)

Serves 8

1	9 inch *unbaked* pie crust (store-bought or see Memorable Pie Crust recipe)
2	cups sweet potatoes, cooked, mashed
2	eggs, slightly beaten
3/4	cup sugar
1/2	teaspoon salt
1/2	teaspoon ginger
1/2	teaspoon nutmeg
1	teaspoon vanilla
1	tablespoon rum
1 2/3	cups evaporated milk
1/2	cup margarine

1. Bake or boil peeled sliced potatoes until tender. Mash to measure. No lumps, please.

2.   Preheat oven to 400° F.
3.   Combine all ingredients. Pour into *unbaked* pie crust.

Pecan Topping

1/4   cup margarine
1/2   cup brown sugar
1/3   cup flour
1/2   teaspoon cinnamon
1/2   cup broken pecans

1.   Combine margarine, brown sugar, flour, and cinnamon. Blend well. Stir in pecans. Sprinkle on top of pie.
2.   Bake pie for 50 minutes of until knife inserted comes out clean.

Outrageous Strawberry Pie

1   9 inch baked pie crust (store-bought or see Memorable Pie Crust recipe)
2   pints fresh strawberries
3/4-1   cup water
3/4   cup sugar
3   tablespoons cornstarch
Whisper of salt
Lime juice
1   pint heavy whipping cream

1.   Place bowl and beaters in freezer to be used to whip cream.
2.   Wash berries and remove about 1 cup bruised ones for sauce. Blenderize these berries in 3/4 cup water until smooth.
3.   In sauce pan, mix sugar, cornstarch, and salt. To this slowly add berry mixture stirring constantly so it won't lump. Cook over medium to medium-high heat, stirring constantly until thick. Remove from heat. Stir in lime juice. Cool in refrigerator.
4.   Slice remaining berries into halves or thirds. Dry as well as possible.
5.   In your icy bowl whip cream until stiff. Don't over do and make butter, but it must be stiff. Set aside 1 cup whipped cream.
6.   Gently fold cold berry mixture and berries into whipped cream. Pour into *baked* shell. Top with remaining cup of whipped cream. Refrigerate 2 hours before serving. Store chilled.

Fresh Blueberry Pie

Serves 6-8

When blueberries are in season, be sure not to miss this pie.

1   9 inch baked pie crust (store-bought or see Memorable Pie Crust recipe)
2   pints fresh blueberries
3/4   cup sugar
3   tablespoons and 1 teaspoon cornstarch
1/8   teaspoon salt
1/4   cup water
2   tablespoons butter, *no substitutes*
1-4   tablespoons fresh lime juice

1.   Wash and drain blueberries *very well*. Even if you have to spread them on paper towels to get off excess water. This is so crust won't get soggy.
2.   Mix sugar, salt, and cornstarch in a sauce pan until well blended. Add water and 2 cups blueberries. Cook over medium heat stirring constantly until mixture is thick and clear. Remove from heat, add butter and lime juice, 1 tablespoon at a time. I use all 4 tablespoons, but you can taste the lime then. Lime juice gives it zip. Let cool until warm.
3.   Pour fresh berries into *baked* pie shell and pour berry mixture on top.

Unbelievable!

Wild Elderberry Crisp

Serves 6

Florida Elder is commonly seen growing along roadsides, fences, and pond banks as far north as Louisiana. The shrub reaches a height of about fifteen feet with tiny white fragrant flowers growing in large flat-topped clusters. Glossy black berries are about one eighth inch in diameter. Unripe berries and leaves are toxic! Again, I can't stress enough how important it is to know wild plants. Recommended reading: Living Off The Land by Marian Van Atta, and Florida Wild Flowers, by C. Ritchie Bell and Bryan Taylor. This recipe is compliments of naturalist Roger Hammer.

3   cups fully ripe elderberries
1-1/2   cups water
1-2   teaspoons lime juice to taste
1/4   teaspoon nutmeg to taste
1/2   cup sugar to taste
2   tablespoons cornstarch

1	cup flour
1	cup sugar
1/2	cup margarine

1. Preheat oven to 350° F.
2. Wash berries, remove all stems. Use only *ripe* unblemished fruit. Pour fruit into a pan and add 1-1 1/2 cups water. Add lime juice, nutmeg, and sugar to taste. Mix corn starch with a small amount of water. Add slowly so it won't lump. Cook, stirring constantly until sugar is dissolved and mixture thick. Pour into 9 x 9 inch greased square pan.
3. Topping—with a mixer blend flour, sugar, and margarine until crumbly. Pour on berries. Bake 35-40 minutes, until brown and crisp.

Greek Butter Cookies

Yields 2-3 dozen

2	cups unsalted butter, *no substitutes*
3/4	cup confectioners sugar, sifted
1/2	teaspoon baking powder
1	egg
1 1/2	teaspoons Cognac
4 1/2	cups pastry flour, sifted twice
Whole cloves	
Powdered sugar	

1. Preheat oven to 350° F.
2. In a large mixing bowl, beat butter until very light. Mix in sugar and baking powder, then egg and Cognac. Add flour. This may have to be worked in with your hands.
3. Form into ovals (if too sticky, refrigerate). Place on greased cookie sheet. Press a whole clove into the center of each one.
4. Bake for 15 minutes. Do not brown. Roll in sifted confectioners sugar.

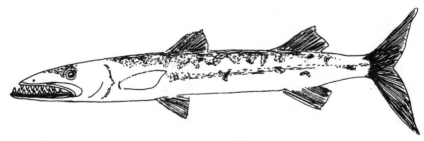

Barracuda

Hidden Treasure Cookies

Yields 2 dozen

1	cup butter, *no substitutes*
1	teaspoon vanilla
2	cups flour
1/2	teaspoon salt
1	cup rolled oats—not instant oatmeal
12	ounce package cream cheese

Approximately 1/4 cup your favorite preserves

1. Preheat oven to 425° F.
2. In a large mixing bowl cream butter and vanilla. Blend in flour, salt, and oats. Then cream cheese. Chill in refrigerator.
3. Roll out on a floured surface to 1/4 inch thickness. Cut into 2 inch squares. Fill center with about 1/2 teaspoon of preserves. Bring up the four corners and pinch together.
4. Bake on ungreased cookie sheet for 10-12 minutes.

Alice's Borrowed Molasses Snaps

Yields 4 dozen

Alice and I were great neighbors for years. She never kept molasses in her larder. I, on the other hand, always have it in case of a sweet tooth attack. It is a great emergency ration eaten directly from the spoon. Whenever I would see Alice heading my way with an empty measuring cup, I knew I was in for a treat. These thin crispy cookies taste like the traditional ginger snap.

3/4	cup margarine, softened
1	cup light brown sugar, firmly packed
1	large egg
1/4	cup molasses
1/4	teaspoon salt
2	teaspoons baking soda
1	teaspoon cinnamon
1	teaspoon ginger
1/4	teaspoon cloves
2 1/2	cups flour

Granulated sugar

1. In a large mixing bowl, with an electric mixer, cream margarine and brown sugar. Add all remaining ingredients in order given except granulated sugar. When thoroughly blended, chill one hour in refrigerator.

2.   Preheat oven to 375° F.
3.   Roll cookies into balls about the size of walnuts, then roll in granulated sugar. Bake 10-12 minutes.

The Snowy Egret has white plumage, black beak and legs, and yellow feet.

Spicy Oatmeal Cookies

Yields 5-6 dozen

1	cup margarine, softened
1 1/2	cups sugar
2	cups uncooked old-fashioned oatmeal (not instant)
1	cup sour cream
1	teaspoon baking soda
1/2	teaspoon baking powder
2	cups flour
2	teaspoons cinnamon
1/4	teaspoon each, cloves, allspice, and ginger
1/8	teaspoon nutmeg
1	cup broken nuts (I like walnuts)
1	cup raisins, plumped (optional)

1.   Preheat oven to 350° F. Grease cookie sheets first time only.
2.   Plumping raisins isn't necessary, but brings out the flavor. Fill a small pan with hot water, toss in raisins, bring to a boil, let raisins sit 5 minutes. Drain raisins well in a strainer or colander.
3.   In a large mixing bowl with an electric mixer, cream margarine and sugar, add all remaining ingredients in order given, and stir in nuts and raisins last.
4.   Drop dough onto cookie sheet, about 1 tablespoon per cookie. They spread so give them room. Bake 20-25 minutes or until done.

Ghosts and Goblins
(Pumpkin Cookies)

Yields about 48 cookies

1/2 cup margarine
1   cup brown sugar, firmly packed
1   cup pumpkin
2   eggs beaten
2   cups sifted flour
4   teaspoons baking powder
1/2   teaspoon nutmeg
1/4   teaspoon ginger
1   tablespoon cinnamon
1   teaspoon salt
1   cup raisins
1   cup broken nuts

1. Preheat oven to 350° F.
2. In a large mixing bowl, cream shortening, add sugar, beat until light and fluffy. Blend in pumpkin and eggs.
3. Sift dry ingredients. Blend into pumpkin mixture. Stir in nuts and raisins.
4. Drop by teaspoon onto a greased cookie sheet. Bake approximately 11 minutes or until lightly browned. These freeze well.

Chocolate Chocolate Chip Cookies

Yields 6 dozen

1   cup margarine, softened
1   cup sugar
1/2   cup brown sugar, firmly packed
1   teaspoon vanilla
1   egg
2   tablespoons milk
1/2   teaspoon baking soda
1/2   cup Hershey's powdered cocoa
1/2   teaspoon salt
1 3/4   cups flour
12   ounce package semi sweet chocolate chips
1/2   cup broken walnuts

1. Preheat oven to 350° F.
2. Cream margarine and sugars in a large mixing bowl. Add remaining ingredients except chips and nuts, blend well. Mix in chips and nuts.
3. Drop by teaspoons onto a lightly greased cookie sheet. Allow room for spreading.
4. Bake 12 minutes.

Sinful Cookies

Yields about 50 cookies

1 cup margarine
1 cup sugar
1 egg, separated
2 cups flour
1 teaspoon cinnamon
1 teaspoon vanilla
1 cup chopped walnuts

1. Preheat oven to 350° F.
2. In a large mixing bowl beat margarine, sugar and egg yolk. Blend in flour, cinnamon, and vanilla.
3. Pat dough into a well-greased shallow flat pan—about 15 x 10 inch x 1 inch.
4. Beat 1 tablespoon water into egg white until frothy. Spread onto dough. Top with walnuts. Press walnuts down into dough.
5. Bake 20-25 minutes. Cut into squares while warm.

Merman's Shaving Brush is an algae.

Cheese Cake Cookie Squares

Yields 16 squares

These are a great breakfast treat on sailing trips.

1/3 cup margarine
1/3 cup light brown sugar, firmly packed
1 cup flour
1/2 cup chopped walnuts
1/4 cup sugar
8 ounce package cream cheese, room temperature
1 egg
2 tablespoons milk
1-3 tablespoons lime juice (to taste)
1/2 teaspoon vanilla

1. Preheat oven to 350° F. Grease 8 x 8 inch square pan.
2. In a large mixing bowl, cream margarine and brown sugar with an electric mixer, then add flour and walnuts. Mixture should be some-what crumbly. Set aside one cup of mixture, press remainder into bottom of cake pan.
3. Bake about 12 minutes.
4. Beat sugar and cream cheese in a mixing bowl until well blended. Beat in egg, milk, lime juice to taste, and vanilla. Spread over crust. Top with remaining crumb mixture.
5. Return to oven for another 25 minutes. Cut into squares while warm. Store in refrigerator.

Pecan Date Cookies

Yields 16 squares

2 eggs
1/2 cup sugar
1 teaspoon vanilla
1/2 cup flour, sifted
1/2 teaspoon baking powder
1/2 teaspoon salt
1 cup broken pecans
2 cups dates, chopped
3/4 cup confectioners sugar, sifted

1. Preheat oven to 325° F. Grease an 8 x 8 inch square pan.
2. In a large mixing bowl, beat eggs until foamy with an electric mixer. Add sugar and vanilla. Blend well.

3.   Add flour, baking powder, and salt. Mix well. Stir in pecans and dates.
4.   Pour into prepared pan. Bake 25-30 minutes or until top is dull.
5.   Cut into squares while warm. Roll in confectioners sugar. Cool. Roll again.

Rum Balls

Yields 70-80

5   cups Vanilla Wafer crumbs
1   cup dark rum* or more
1/4   cup and 2 tablespoons light corn syrup
2   cups chopped walnuts or pecans
1/4   cup Hershey's powdered cocoa
1   box powdered sugar, sifted

1.   Whiz Vanilla Wafers in a food processor or crush in a bag with a rolling pin until fine. Do the same for the nuts. Mix all ingredients except powdered sugar. Add more rum if desired.
2.   Form into walnut sized balls. Roll in powdered sugar. Store in covered container to mellow.

*Your favorite liquor may be substituted for rum.

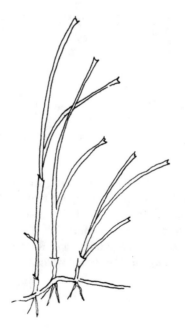

Cuban Shoal Weed has jagged tops and is often found with manatee grass which has rounded tops.

Chocolate Peanut Butter Delights

Yields about 7 dozen

This is another one of my mother's sinful concoctions.

1/2 cup margarine
2   cups creamy peanut butter
1   pound confectioners sugar
3   cups Rice Krispies
12   ounce package semi sweet chocolate chips
2/3 bar paraffin wax*

1. In a medium sauce pan melt margarine with peanut butter. Blend well.
2. Sift confectioners sugar. Blend into peanut butter mixture. Add Rice Krispies, working with hands if necessary.
3. Form into about 1 inch balls.
4. In a double boiler or over very low heat in a sauce pan, melt paraffin and chocolate, stirring constantly. Don't wander away, chocolate directly over heat burns easily. When smooth, with tongs begin dipping balls. Set out on waxed paper to harden. Chill or freeze.

*Wax is used in chocolate to help it keep its shape in warm weather.

Crunchy Peanut Butter Fudge

1/2 cup margarine
1   pound box light brown sugar
1/2 cup milk
3/4 cup crunchy peanut butter
1   pound confectioners sugar
1   teaspoon vanilla
1/2 cup broken peanuts

1. In a medium sauce pan melt margarine, stir in brown sugar, and milk. Bring to a rolling boil, stirring constantly for two minutes.
2. Remove from heat. Stir in peanut butter and vanilla, then confectioners sugar. Beat until smooth. Stir in peanuts.
3. Spread into greased 9 inch square pan. Refrigerate until set. Cut into squares. Serve with a large pitcher of ice water.

Sour Cream Fudge

Yields 36 pieces

2 cups sugar
2 tablespoons Light Karo syrup
1/4 cup Hershey's powdered cocoa
1/2 cup sour cream
1/2 cup margarine
1/2 teaspoon vanilla
1/2 cup broken walnuts

1. In a sauce pan combine all ingredients except vanilla and nuts. Cook over medium-high heat about 4 minutes. A small drop of chocolate in water should form a soft ball (234° F - 238° F on a candy thermometer). A soft ball flattens slightly when dropped into cold water.
2. Remove pan from heat. Set in sink filled with a couple inches of cold water for 2 minutes. Then add nuts and vanilla. Beat with an electric mixer. It will go from shiny to satiny. Pour into an 8 inch x 8 inch greased pan. Refrigerate.

The American Egret has a yellow beak, black legs and feet, and white plumage.

Four Minute Microwave Fudge

Yields 36 pieces

1 box confectioners sugar, sifted
1/2 cup Hershey's Powdered Baking Cocoa
1/2 cup margarine
1/4 cup plus 1 tablespoon milk
1/2 cup broken walnuts

1. Combine all ingredients in a large glass mixing bowl. Microwave on high 4 minutes. Beat with an electric mixer until well blended.
2. Pour in an 8 inch square, well-greased baking dish. Cover and refrigerate. Store in refrigerator.

Sugar and Spice Pecans

Yields 2 1/2 cups

2 1/2	cups pecan halves
1	cup sugar
1/ 2	cup water
1	teaspoon cinnamon
1	teaspoon salt
1 1/2	teaspoon vanilla

1. Preheat oven to 375° F.
2. Toast pecans for about 15 minutes stirring often. Cool.
3. In a medium/large sauce pan combine sugar, water, cinnamon, and salt. Cook over medium-high heat to soft ball stage (236° F) without stirring. Soft ball means a bit of sugar mixture dropped into a glass of water forms a slightly flattened ball. Remove from heat. Add vanilla and pecans. Stir until mixture becomes creamy.
4. Pour onto a greased cookie sheet and separate into small portions.

Becky's Mud Puppy Mousse

Serves 8-10

2	tablespoons unflavored gelatin
1/2	cup Creme de Cacao
6	ounces semi-sweet baking chocolate
1/4	cup water
1	pint heavy whipping cream
6	egg whites

Whisper of salt

1/2	cup sugar
1/2	cup toasted slivered almonds
1	cup crumbled almond macaroons
1	package ladyfingers

A few drops vanilla flavoring

1. Put deep bowl and beaters in freezer to chill for whipping cream.
2. In a sauce pan combine gelatin, Creme e Cacao, 4 ounces baking chocolate, and 1/4 cup water. Melt over low heat, stirring so it blends and doesn't burn. Refrigerate to cool.
3. Beat whipping cream in chilled bowl until stiff. Refrigerate.
4. Wash beaters well in hot soapy water. Beat egg whites until stiff. Gradually add sugar and salt.

5.   Fold together egg whites and all but 2/3 cup whipping cream. (to be reserved for topping). Then fold in melted chocolate. Fold in almonds and macaroons. Refrigerate mousse and 2/3 cup whipped cream.

6.   Line the sides of a 1 1/2 quart bowl with ladyfingers. Grate 1 ounce chocolate and cover bottom. Pour chocolate mousse mixture into center. Cover with plastic wrap and refrigerate at least 2 hours.

7.   Flavor remaining 2/3 cup whipped cream with vanilla to taste. Unmold mousse. Top with whipped cream and more grated chocolate.

Yes, it is worth all the trouble!

Strawberry Fool

Serves 4-6

This simple, delicious dessert of the Caribbean Islands is said to be so easy to fix, a fool can make it, hence the name. Other fresh fruits may be substituted for strawberries, such as mango, pineapple, kiwi, and peaches.

2   cups fresh strawberries, chopped
1   cup heavy whipping cream
1-4 tablespoons confectioners sugar
1   teaspoon vanilla extract

1.   Chill bowl and beaters in freezer 15 minutes. Chilled serving bowls* are optional, but nice.

2.   Place fresh fruit in a large sieve or colander to drain.

3.   Pour whipping cream into chilled bowl and whip with electric mixer until thick. Add vanilla and sugar to taste. Whip until stiff.

4.   Carefully fold in fruit, serve at once.

*I like to serve mine in chilled wine glasses. It's different!

Branham's Tulip is beige with brown bands.

Fresh Coconut Sherbet

Yields about 3 to 4 cups

Try to use fresh coconut for this spectacular treat.

1   coconut
2   cups hot milk
1/8 teaspoon cream of tartar
1   cup sugar
1/4 cup water
Almond extract
1/2 cup broken walnuts

1.   Remove coconut from shell (see Coconut Palm for husking instructions).
2.   In a food processor, blender or with a grater, coarsely chop 1 cup coconut and set aside or 1 cup commercially prepared shredded coconut. Blenderize the rest of the nut as fine as possible and add to 2 cups hot milk. Let rest 15-30 minutes.
3.   In a small sauce pan, combine cream of tartar, sugar, and water, bring to a boil, stirring until sugar is dissolved and solution is completely clear. Let cool.
4.   Pour coconut liquid into a fine meshed sieve and press out as much liquid as possible into a mixing bowl.
5.   Combine coconut milk and syrup, blend well. Add 1 or 2 drops almond extract, and stir in walnuts and 1 cup chopped coconut.
6.   Pour into a shallow freezer-proof container. Stir about every 1/2 hour (for about the first 2 hours) to keep it from freezing solid.

Biscayne Bay Pears

Serves 2 halves per person

This is quite wonderful and easily prepared on a boat.

1   can pear halves (any size can)
1   teaspoon coconut per pear half
1   teaspoon walnuts per pear half
1   teaspoon raisins per pear half
Orange or calamondin marmalade
Hershey's chocolate syrup (in a can)

1.   Mix coconut, walnuts, and raisins. Use enough marmalade to bind the mixture together. Stuff the center of each pear.
2.   Warm the chocolate syrup over low heat. Pour over pears.

Flambéed Rum Walnut Sauce

Yields 3 cups

Served over vanilla ice cream or frozen yogurt, this simple dessert becomes elegant.

2   cups light brown sugar, packed
1   cup water
1/2 cup rum
8   ounce package pitted dates, chopped
1   cup broken walnuts

1.   In a medium sauce pan, boil water and sugar 20 minutes, stirring occasionally. Add dates, nuts, and 1/4 cup rum. Cool. Pour into a jar with a tight-fitting lid. Store in refrigerator. This will keep several weeks.
2.   To serve, warm sauce. Heat remaining 1/4 cup rum. When serving, pour sauce over ice cream. Ignite rum. Pour over sauce.

The Great White Heron has a yellow beak, yellow-green legs, and white plumage.

Native Butterfly Orchid

Hidden Treasure

Mangoes

Step 1

Step 2

Step3

Mango—The Tropical Peach

Mangoes, native to Southeast Asia, were established in the West Indies by the mid 1700s and arrived in Florida by the 1830s. As a tropical fruit, they are surpassed in consumption only by bananas and coconuts.

The mango is everything the fuzzy-skinned peach wishes it could be. This smooth-skinned, pendulous fruit ranges in color from a satiny cool green tinged in purple, to a gaudy yellow splashed with red. Larger than a peach, mangoes can weigh several pounds. However, their true beauty lies within.

Mango flesh is exotic, golden to deep orange, its scent and taste heavy with a sweet perfume. It is erotic. So slippery and juicy, it is said to be best eaten naked in a bathtub. This fruit is sinful because you can never get enough and wicked because its sap may cause blisters on your skin. Had the Garden of Eden been in the tropics, no doubt that Eve would have seduced Adam with a mango.

Legend claims that seventeenth century Latin American revolutions were planned to coincide with mango season so the rebels would have enough to eat. Floridians harvest mangoes from late May to early October. Most mangoes ripen from the seed out and should be harvested before fully ripe.

Before picking a mango, check the running sap at the base of the stem. Milky sap indicates it is not quite ready. Clear sap means the fruit can be taken, but pick it carefully, directing the fruit away from your face. Sap spray can cause mango poisoning, a poison ivy-like rash.

Green mangoes rich in vitamin C, taste like apples when cooked. The golden flesh of ripe fruit is high in vitamin A.

Today, over 200 cultivated varieties of mangoes are grown in Florida. Less than a dozen are commercially produced. Years ago the most common mango was the "Turpentine." It tasted like an ultra sweet peach marinated in turpentine. Its flesh was fibrous and stringy and hung in your teeth like orange dental floss.

In 1902 a Coconut Grove resident, Captain John J. Haden, crossed a Mulgoba and a Turpentine, ultimately creating the Haden mango. This fruit was so superior that as a child I can clearly remember my first taste. I recall my grandmother cupping the large aromatic fruit in her hand and with great reverence saying, "This is a Haden." So we all gathered around while she peeled and sliced the slippery fruit. We tasted. Gone were the turpentine and strings, leaving only the sweet, peachy, perfumy, golden fruit we take for granted today. Truly, the mango is a peach touched by magic.

Mango Slicing Made Easy (See Illustrations to the Left)
1. With a long sharp knife, going in as close to the seed as possible, slice off each cheek. You will have three sections. Get a grip on the fruit and carefully score it down to the skin.

2. Pick the scored fruit up in both hands and push up from the bottom (skin side) with both thumbs, turning the fruit inside out. Slice or bite off the cubes.
3. Peel the skin off the seed section and slice around the seed to create wedges. Cut around seed and enjoy the last of your fruit, noting that 1/2 cup of sliced mango is equal to about 54 calories.

Mango Chutney

Yields 8 pints

4	cups chopped mangoes, part green, part ripe
3	green peppers, finely chopped
1	large onion, chopped (about 3 or more inches in diameter)
1	tablespoon hot chili peppers, with seeds, finely chopped
1	clove garlic, crushed
1	tablespoon salt
1	one pound box, light brown sugar
1/2	pound seedless raisins
1	cup grapefruit juice
1	cup cider vinegar
1	tablespoon white mustard seed
1	teaspoon ground ginger
2	teaspoons each allspice, cloves, and cinnamon
2 1/4	ounce package sliced almonds

1.   In a 4-quart pot, combine first six ingredients, stir gently, let rest one hour. Drain off liquid.
2.   Add all remaining ingredients, bring to a boil, reduce heat to medium medium-low, about 30 minutes. Stir and watch carefully—this can burn. While hot, pour into sterilized jars, leaving about 1/2 inch space at top. Cap tightly. Cool. Tighten caps.
3.   Serve as an accompaniment to curry dishes.

Mango Preserves

Yields four 1/2 pints

4	cups fully ripe mangoes finely chopped by hand or food processor
2	tablespoons lime juice
4	cups sugar
1	package Sure-Jel

1.   In a large sauce pan, mix mangoes with lime juice and Sure-Jel. Place over high heat. When it comes to a full boil, add sugar. Bring to a full rolling boil

for 1 minute (this cannot be stirred down). Remove from heat, skim off foam. Continue to stir and skim for five minutes to cool slightly.
2.   Ladle into sterilized jars. Cap or cover with paraffin. Cool. Tighten caps.

Pineapple Mango Jam

Yields six to seven 1/2 pints

2   quarts mangoes, finely cut or chopped in a food processor
4   cups sugar
20   ounce can crushed pineapple in its own juice
1/4 cup lime juice

1.   Place all ingredients in a large sauce pan. Cook rapidly stirring occasionally until sugar is melted and the mixture thickens, about 1 hour. Skim off foam during cooking.
2.   Ladle into sterilized glasses. Cap or cover with paraffin. Cool. Tighten caps.

Guava Jelly

Yields two 8 ounce jars

Pick unblemished fruit. Include a fair number of green guavas—green fruit contains a greater amount of pectin which makes jelly jell. The key to making good jelly is to use as little water as possible. Cooking jelly in large amounts results in a darker color and an inferior product, as it takes longer to boil. This jelly is worth all the trouble.

Wash and slice guavas. Put just enough water in the pan to cover them. Cook until soft. Cool. Strain through a clean cloth. I use an old pillow case.

Jelly
1   cup guava juice
1   cup sugar
1   tablespoon Key lime juice

1.   Put ingredients into a large pot. Jelly has a tendency to boil up high in the pot. Cook on medium-high, bring to a boil, and stir occasionally for about 10 minutes.
2.   Pour into sterilized jars and seal with lid or paraffin.

Calamondin Marmalade

Yields 2 jars

Calamondins are the hardiest of all citrus. They are a cross between a tangerine and a kumquat, and look and smell like tiny oranges. Eaten fresh, they are very sour, however the marmalade is superb.

About 20 calamondins equal 1 cup fruit mixture

1. Wash and halve fruit. Remove seeds. Put fruit into a food processor. You're not looking for a puree, but a uniform consistency.
2. Pour into pot, cover with water. Simmer the fruit about 45 minutes.

Marmalade
1   cup fruit mixture
1   cup sugar

1. Pour ingredients into a large pot. Marmalade boils high up into the pot. Bring it to a boil on medium-high, stirring so it won't burn. Cooking time varies with amount, but all sugar must be dissolved.
2. Pour into sterilized jars. Cover with paraffin or if using canning jars, cool. Tighten caps.

Spiked Cranberry Relish

Yields 3 cups

1   12 ounce package fresh cranberries
1   orange
1   cup sugar
1   tablespoon Triple Sec
3   tablespoons Chambord (raspberry liqueur)

1. Cut orange into quarters. Remove seeds. Wash cranberries. Put cranberries and orange sections into food processor and whiz. Mix in remaining ingredients. Test for sweetness. Add more sugar if necessary. Serve chilled.

The Green Turtle has green body fat, a brown shell and can weigh from 100-200 pounds.

Tropical Barbecue Sauce

Yields about 1 cup

This sauce is spicy hot and will take your breath away.

1/2 cup vinegar
1/4 cup catsup
1   tablespoon sugar
1   tablespoon dry mustard
1/2 teaspoon or less Tabasco sauce
1/2 teaspoon or less black pepper
1/2 teaspoon salt
1/2 teaspoon paprika
2   tablespoons fresh onion, minced
Juice of 2 calamondins or one lemon
2   tablespoons Worcestershire sauce

Combine all ingredients in a small sauce pan, bring to a boil, reduce heat. Simmer 15-30 minutes. Serve warm over chicken, fish, chops or hamburgers.

Buccaneer Barbecue Sauce

Yields 1 quart

1   cup margarine
1   cup onion, minced
1   clove garlic, crushed
1   cup catsup
1   cup chili sauce
1/2 cup cider vinegar
1/2 cup brown sugar, packed
1   tablespoon horseradish
2   tablespoons Worcestershire sauce
1   tablespoon mustard
1   tablespoon liquid smoke
1   tablespoon salt
Several dashes Tabasco sauce

In a medium sauce pan simmer onion in margarine until soft. Add remaining ingredients. Simmer about 15 minutes. Refrigerate. Keeps several months. Use on chicken, ribs, and other meats.

Honey Garlic Sauce

Yields about 2/3 cup
or enough for 4 chicken breasts

Use on Snap Cackle And Pop Oven-Fried Chicken.

1/2　cup water
1　　teaspoon cornstarch
3　　cloves garlic, crushed
3　　tablespoons plus 1 teaspoon sugar
2　　teaspoons vinegar
3　　tablespoons plus 1 teaspoon honey
1　　teaspoon margarine

Dissolve cornstarch in a teaspoon of water. Mix with all remaining ingredients. Bring to a boil until thickened. Pour over oven fried chicken. Serve warm.

The Loggerhead Turtle has a reddish-brown shell and usually weighs under 300 pounds.

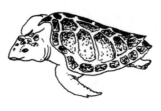

Pineapple Sauce

Yields about 1 cup for 4-6 breasts

8　　ounce can crushed pineapple in its own juice
2　　teaspoons yellow mustard
2　　tablespoons lemon juice

Combine all ingredients. Cook over low heat about 5-8 minutes. Pour over cooked chicken.

Garlic Butter Sauce

Yield 1/4 cup

1　　clove garlic
1/4　cup butter or margarine

Crush garlic. Melt margarine over low heat, add garlic. Allow flavors to blend over heat about 5 minutes. Do not burn!

The Ridley Turtle has a gray shell and is the smalles sea turtle under 100 pounds

The Hawksbill Turtle has a brown patterned shell with overlaping scales and weighs 30 to 100 pounds.

Lime Butter Sauce

Yield 1/4 cup

1/4	cup butter or margarine
1 1/2	tablespoons Key lime juice (or regular lime)
2	dashes Tabasco sauce

Melt margarine. Add lime and Tabasco. Serve on seafood, chicken or greens.

Honey Butter

Yield 1/2 cup

1/2	cup butter or margarine
1/3-1/2	cup honey

Soften butter. Cream honey slowly into butter. Refrigerate. Great on biscuits.

Apple Orange Topping

Yields 1 cup for 4-6 breasts

2	Granny Smith apples, peeled and thinly sliced
1	large orange, peeled and cut up, no seeds
1/8	teaspoon ground cloves
1/4	cup water

Combine all ingredients in a saucepan. Simmer for 10 minutes. Use as a topping on baked chicken.

Red Snapper Sauce

Yields 2 cups

1/2	cup tomato paste
1/2	cup olive oil
1/2	cup wine vinegar
1/2	cup tarragon vinegar
1 1/2	tablespoons Worcestershire sauce
1 1/2	tablespoons paprika
1 1/2	teaspoons black pepper

Whisper each of oregano and cardamom
Sugar to taste

Blend all ingredients. Pour into a clean bottle. Store in refrigerator. Serve on fish.

Shrimp Cocktail Sauce

3/4 cup commercially prepared chili sauce
1/4 cup catsup
1   fresh lime
1-4 tablespoons hot horseradish
Wedges of lime
Lettuce
Crackers

1.   Mix chili sauce and catsup, add lime juice and horseradish to taste.
2.   Line individual bowls with lettuce leaves, arrange shrimp around edges, spoon sauce in center. Garnish with lime wedge. Serve chilled with crackers.

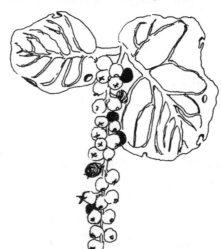

Seagrape

Bleu Cheese Dressing

Yields about 1 cup

1   cup sour cream or yogurt or a combination
1/2 teaspoon salt
1/2 teaspoon dry mustard
1/2 tablespoon fresh onion, minced
2   ounces bleu cheese, crumbled
Milk (optional)

Combine all ingredients. If too thick for your taste, thin with milk. Store in refrigerator. Serve on salads, as a dip for fresh vegetables, or with Grilled Outdoor Chicken and Tropical Barbecue Sauce.

The Leatherback Turtle has a gray-blue shell with five long ridges and no scales, and weighs from 700 to 1600 pounds.

Pesto Coconut Grove

Yields 1 cup

1/2 cup packed fresh basil leaves
1/2 cup packed fresh parsley
1/4 cup walnuts
1/4 cup Parmesan cheese
2   large garlic cloves
1/2 cup olive oil
Salt and pepper

1.   Using a blender or food processor, blend basil, parsley, walnuts, parmesan, and garlic cloves. Leave processor on and slowly pour in oil. Blend until smooth. Add salt and pepper to taste. If pesto is too thick, add olive oil to thin. Pour into a glass jar. Top with a thin layer of olive oil. Screw on lid.
2.   Serve at room temperature over tomatoes or tomato-basil pasta.

Wild Peppergrass Vinegar

Some people might call peppergrass a weed. I call it a native plant. To me a weed is simply a plant out of place. In Puerto Rico it is used as a remedy for liver trouble. The zippy hot, mustard-flavored leaves can be cooked or served in salads. This hardy plant grows wild all over the United States and Caribbean. It is easy to identify, but if you're not certain that you're picking peppergrass, give a piece to a trustworthy person in case they need to show it to the fire rescue team. Your treatment and recovery will be speeded tremendously if they know the culprit straight away. Now bite off a hunk. Does it taste similar to green pepper or mustard greens with a real kick? Relax, you've got the right plant.

12 or so peppergrass seed spikes
Peppergrass leaves
1   cup cider vinegar
1-2 red chili peppers
A small bottle with cap. A 10 ounce seltzer water bottle works nicely.

1. Push your seed spikes and some leaves into the bottle.
2. Chilis are optional. Do you like it hot? Throw them in.
3. Pour in vinegar. Cap and store in a dark place for two weeks. Use as you would any flavored vinegar.

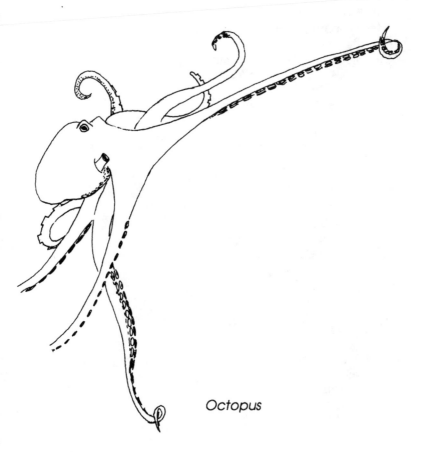

Octopus

Vanilla Extract

Yields 1 cup

1   cup inexpensive brandy
2   vanilla beans, cut up

Pour into a small bottle, add vanilla beans. Seal. Shake once a week. Let age 3 months. Brandy can be replenished as used once it is aged. After 1/2 cup has been replenished, add another vanilla bean.

Old Sour

Yields 1 cup

Pioneers used this as a table seasoning for meat and seafood.

1-1 1/2   teaspoons salt
1   cup Key lime Juice
1   chili pepper (optional)

Combine all ingredients. Pour into a bottle. Cap. Age for 2-4 weeks or until fermentation ceases.

Tail Waggin' Dog Soup

Kitchen Scraps
    Potato peels
    Green bean ends
    Chicken skins
    Meat scraps

Liquid
    Water from canned veggies
    Liquid from cooking

Leftovers
    Anything nourishing hanging around in the refrigerator

Combine vegetable scraps, liquid, leftovers. Simmer until tender. Cool. Pour over dog food. Serve to your best friend and loyal canine companion.

Wooky Cookies
(Gourmet Dog Biscuits)

Yields about 40 biscuits

1	package yeast
1/4	cup warm water
3 1/2	cups flour
3	cups whole wheat flour
2	cups wheat germ
1	cup yellow corn meal
1/2	teaspoon garlic powder
1/2	cup non fat dry milk powder
1	tablespoon salt
3	cups beef or chicken broth
1	beef bouillon cube
1	egg

1.   Preheat oven to 300° F.
2.   Dissolve yeast in water. Allow to set about 10 minutes.
3.   Mix flours, wheat germ, cornmeal, garlic powder, dry milk, and salt. Work in yeast mixture and broth. This is stiff. Let it rest 5 minutes—you too.
4.   Roll out to 1/4 inch thick. Use your cookie cutters. Dogs prefer cat shapes, moons, trees, rabbits. I even have a bone shape.
5.   Place on greased cookie sheet 1 inch apart.
6.   Dissolve beef bouillon cube in 1 tablespoon warm water. Mix with beaten egg. Brush top of biscuits with this mixture.
7.   Bake for 45 minutes. Turn off heat. Leave in oven overnight to harden. Store in air-tight container.

Gator's Magic Bubble Soap

Yields 1/3 cup

*My pup Gator played a key role in the research and development of this recipe.
This self-appointed "Bubble Assassin," took no prisoners. When the enemy
became so numerous and even Gator couldn't keep up, I knew the formula was
right.*

3	tablespoons water
2	tablespoons new Dawn Liquid Detergent
1	teaspoon Karo syrup
1	bubble wand

Combine all ingredients and blow.

Edible Peanut Butter Clay

Yields about 1 cup
Entertains 2-3

3/4 cup instant non-fat dry milk powder
3/4 cup smooth peanut butter
1/4 cup honey plus 2 tablespoons
Raisins, nuts, sugar sprinkles for decoration

1. In a mixing bowl work powdered milk into peanut butter until smooth.
Add honey and a bit more if necessary to get a clay like consistency.
2. Divide into as many children as you have—no more than 3 please. This
hampers creativity. Set them up with toothpicks for tools, nuts, and raisins for
decorations. The young artists may eat their sculptures. Supervise!

Home Made Clay Dough

Yields 1 cup

1   cup flour
1/2 cup salt
2   teaspoons cream of tartar
1   cup water
1   tablespoon oil
1   teaspoon vanilla
Food coloring

1. In a medium sauce pan blend dry ingredients. Add 1 cup water, stir until
smooth. Add oil, vanilla, and food coloring. Cook until thick and lumpy.
2. Cool on waxed paper. Knead until smooth. Store in plastic bags.

Index

Order Form

Tropical Tastes And Tantalizing Tales, By Carol Garvin

Please mail this order form with payment to: Valiant Press, Inc. P.O. Box 330568, Miami, FL 33233

Number of Copies_____ @ $16.95 $_____
FL residents add 6.5% sales tax $_____
Postage and Handling $_____
(see below)   Total $_____
Ship To:

Name:_____

Address:_____

City:_____State:_____Zip:_____

Daytime Phone:_____
Postage& Handling Fees:$2.00 for 1 copy. Add $ .50 for each additional copy.

Order Form

Tropical Tastes And Tantalizing Tales, By Carol Garvin

Please mail this order form with payment to: Valiant Press, Inc. P.O. Box 330568, Miami, FL 33233

Number of Copies_____ @ $16.95 $_____
FL residents add 6.5% sales tax $_____
Postage and Handling $_____
(see below)   Total $_____
Ship To:

Name:_____

Address:_____

City:_____State:_____Zip:_____

Daytime Phone:_____
Postage& Handling Fees:$2.00 for 1 copy. Add $.50for each additional copy.